Beyond *The Good Earth*

Beyond *The Good Earth*

Transnational Perspectives on Pearl S. Buck

Edited by Jay Cole and John R. Haddad

West Virginia University Press
Morgantown 2019

First edition published 2019 by West Virginia University Press
Printed in the United States of America

ISBN:
Cloth 978-1-946684-77-6
Paper 978-1-946684-75-2
Ebook 978-1-946684-76-9

Library of Congress Cataloging-in-Publication Data
Names: Cole, John J. K., editor. | Haddad, John Rogers, editor. | Pearl S. Buck Living Gateway Conference (2016 : Morgantown, W. Va.)
Title: Beyond The good earth : transnational perspectives on Pearl S. Buck / edited by Jay Cole and John Haddad.
Description: First edition. | Morgantown : West Virginia University Press, 2019. | Features papers from the Pearl S. Buck Living Gateway Conference, held on the WVU campus in Morgantown, West Virginia, September 11-13, 2016. | Includes bibliographical references and index.
Identifiers: LCCN 2018036507| ISBN 9781946684776 (cloth) | ISBN 9781946684752 (pbk.) | ISBN 9781946684769 (ebook)
Subjects: LCSH: Buck, Pearl S. (Pearl Sydenstricker), 1892-1973--Political and social views--Congresses. | Buck, Pearl S. (Pearl Sydenstricker), 1892-1973--Criticism and interpretation--Congresses. | Novelists, American--20th century--Political activity--Congresses. | Novelists, American--20th century--Biography--Congresses. | Women political activists--United States--Biography--Congresses.
Classification: LCC PS3503.U198 Z57 2019 | DDC 813/.52 [B] --dc23
LC record available at https://lccn.loc.gov/2018036507

Cover design by Than Saffel / WVU Press

Contents

Introduction

Jay Cole and John R. Haddad

In the 1990s, one of the two editors of this volume, John Haddad, was just embarking on his career as a college educator. In two separate college classroom settings, he invoked Pearl Buck, the famous (or so he thought) author of *The Good Earth*. During these two encounters with students, he discovered something alarming about her reputation and literary status in that decade. First, in 1994, he stood before a room of Chinese students at Nankai University in the People's Republic of China. Since it was his first day teaching American literature, he asked the students, as an icebreaker, to list the American authors they knew. Though most students regarded the question impassively, a group of engaged female students seated in the front row excitedly rattled off a few names: Mark Twain, Theodore Dreiser, and Ernest Hemingway. Though impressed by the list, he was somewhat surprised by the omission of Pearl Buck, the most famous American author to write specifically on China. "What about Pearl Buck?" he asked as a follow-up. Though aware of Buck, the students explained that no one read her anymore. "We like the American authors who help us understand America," one student ventured. "We have Chinese authors to explain our own culture, so why would we turn to a foreigner?"

Fast forward five years to the University of Texas at Austin. The editor, now working on his doctoral degree in American studies, had developed a novel course—Americans in China; Chinese in America. As the name implies, the course explored both America's influence in China and the experiences of Chinese people living and working in the United States. While going over the syllabus on the first day, the instructor paused in the assigned reading section when he reached Pearl Buck. *The Good Earth* was to play a key role in the class because it possessed double utility: he planned to use the novel to discuss both the American missionary experience in China and the evolving image of China in the United States. "How many people," he asked the class, "have read *The Good Earth*?" After waiting in vain for a single hand to go up, he posed a different question: "How many people know who Pearl Buck was?" After a moment passed, one young woman broke the silence. "I mean, I've heard of her," she said, "if that's what you mean."

At the time, the young instructor recalled being somewhat taken aback by both classroom experiences. After all, he had always regarded Pearl Buck as a household name. Had she really vanished from the radar screens at both Chinese and American colleges? In hindsight, he can see that the apathy of both Chinese and American students made sense. Let's consider the Chinese classroom first. In the early 1990s, China's opening to the world in the Deng Xiaoping era was well underway. But while China had begun to assert itself on the global stage economically, the nation's academic culture lagged behind its commerce. Scholarly conversations revolving around the complex issue of representation—that is, how foreign authors depict Chinese civilization—had not yet happened. Thus, the Chinese student's blunt response fell in line with the times. If one wishes to study America's past, one should read books like *Huckleberry Finn*. If one's goal is to learn about Chinese civilization, one should read the great Chinese writers. There really was no need for anyone to consult Pearl Buck in a Chinese classroom.

American colleges also had little use for Pearl Buck. Though difficult to understand at first, her diminishing relevance becomes comprehensible when we try to answer the following question: what academic department might include *The Good Earth* on a course syllabus in the 1990s? In English departments, courses on American literature tended to assign works that could shed light on domestic themes and topics—slavery, industrialization, urbanization, the West, white-black race relations, and issues of class. An American author's portrayal of life in the Chinese countryside, no matter how nuanced and rich, failed to advance this objective. What about other disciplines, such as Chinese history or Asian studies? Though many colleges offered majors in these areas, the faculty teaching the classes, if they assigned novels at all, likely selected Chinese classics such as *Dream of the Red Chamber* or *Romance of the Three Kingdoms*. Pearl Buck also failed to find an intellectual home in Asian American studies, even though her remarkable life encompassed Asia and America. This field was reserved for American authors of Asian descent, like Maxine Hong Kingston or Amy Tan. Such was the academic landscape in the 1990s. Though no college professor explicitly consigned Pearl Buck to obsolescence, nearly all of them skipped over her when generating reading lists. Thus, it was no wonder that so few students even knew who she was. Pearl Buck had fallen through the cracks of academia.

More than two decades have passed since those classroom experiences and a lot has clearly changed. Globally, China's dramatic rise as a world power has spurred new intellectual conversations inside Chinese universities. Students and scholars alike want to know how other countries perceived them in the past. What is more, the once fierce antiforeign stance of the Communist Party has waned in an era of globalization. In fact, China has become not just less hostile but also increasingly welcoming to foreign people, goods, books, films, and ideas. In this more open intellectual climate, the Chinese are willing to take seriously the insights of a missionary's daughter who observed rural Chinese life a century ago. In an amazing reversal, some Chinese academics are now inclined to value Buck's portrayals of peasant life for their sensitivity and impartiality; they no longer place much trust in the ideologically driven depictions of the countryside penned by Marxist authors after the Communist Revolution of 1949. Indeed, one of the contributors to this volume, Junwei Yao, was so moved by Buck's life and work that he dedicated his career to the study and promotion of her literature.

The academic landscape in the United States also has shifted favorably. In 2005, the president of the American Studies Association, Shelley Fisher Fishkin, announced that the field had taken what she called a "transnational turn." Instead of concentrating exclusively on domestic topics, scholars and educators in the field now explore transnational themes: borders and the people who cross them, American literature read abroad in translation, the experience of expatriate Americans, the exportation of American culture abroad, the importation of world culture into the United States, representations of non-American peoples in the United States, and the image of America that prevails overseas. In sum, a great shift has taken place: the authors, texts, and themes that once languished on the academic periphery now occupy the center. As a part of the reorienting process, scholars have also rediscovered a group of writers once relegated to the academic margins—the cultural interpreters who explain other cultures to American audiences. As the most influential American author ever to write about China, Pearl Buck currently enjoys something of a renaissance. Along with transnationalism, other academic trade winds now fill her sails. Colleges and universities have recently expanded their offerings in women's studies and race and ethnicity. Pearl Buck, who offers sophisticated treatments of both in her literature, not surprisingly has attracted the attention of scholars and teachers.

Clearly, the changing times seem to call for a fresh look at Pearl Buck. An academic world that once dismissed or forgot about her literary contribution now embraces it. But why is a volume of essays coming out at this time and from this institution—West Virginia University? If favorable *global trends* were required to render Buck relevant again, it takes advantageous *local circumstances* to make a book like this one actually happen.

In 2014, Jay Cole learned about ongoing efforts to engage West Virginia University (WVU) with the Pearl S. Buck Birthplace Foundation. The foundation oversees Buck's birthplace in Hillsboro, West Virginia, and owns the Pearl S. Buck Literary Manuscripts Collection. In his role at that time as chief of staff to the WVU president, Cole was one of many people who helped WVU to fulfill its special mission of service to West Virginia as a public, land-grant university. A significant part of this mission is to generate and share new knowledge and insights—knowledge and insights that can be used to solve problems, improve lives, and inspire creativity. Whether reporting research in agriculture and medicine or amplifying achievements in the arts and humanities, WVU takes pride in this mission in all its myriad forms.

Inspired by this mission, Cole and John Cuthbert, director of the West Virginia and Regional History Center at the WVU Libraries, facilitated WVU's entry into a partnership with the Pearl S. Buck Birthplace Foundation and West Virginia Wesleyan College. Kirk Judd represented the birthplace foundation and Brett Miller represented West Virginia Wesleyan College. The partnership has two primary goals: to preserve the Pearl S. Buck Literary Manuscripts Collection as a scholarly resource and to promote the Pearl S. Buck Birthplace as a cultural tourism destination. These goals are firmly embedded in an appreciation for Buck as a West Virginia native and a desire to increase awareness among West Virginians of her global legacy as an author and humanitarian. These are some of the advantageous local circumstances mentioned above.

You are holding in your hands (or reading on a screen) an example of how WVU accomplishes its public, land-grant mission, in this case through the WVU Press: a book that we hope generates new knowledge and insights about Buck, a twentieth-century stateswoman who occupies a special place at the intersection of writing, politics, human rights, and international relations. We hope this new knowledge and these fresh insights will also help to solve problems, improve lives, and inspire creativity—all things that Buck sought to do during her life and career.

This volume is the culmination of a two-year journey. The journey began in early 2016 with an idea to hold a conference to study the extraordinary life, work, and legacy of Pearl S. Buck. Born in 1892 in the small town of Hillsboro, Pocahontas County, in the eastern mountains of West Virginia, Buck is one of West Virginia's "favorite daughters." She was also the first American woman to win a Nobel Prize for Literature and remains one of only two women (Toni Morrison is the other) to win both a Nobel Prize and a Pulitzer Prize. We hope this book keeps the celebration going, in a sense, and creates new opportunities for scholars, readers, and fans to connect or reconnect around Buck's enduring influence.

After a period of relative obscurity beginning in the 1960s, Buck has enjoyed a resurgence of interest since the 1990s. In 1993, Craig Davidson and Donn Rogosin wrote and produced a documentary, *East Wind, West Wind: Pearl Buck, The Woman Who Embraced the World*. (We are fortunate to have Donn as a contributing author to this volume.) Peter Conn wrote *Pearl S. Buck: A Cultural Biography*, the definitive scholarly biography, in 1996. Later, in 2010, Hilary Spurling penned *Pearl S. Buck in China: A Journey to the Good Earth*. By blazing a trail for the study of Buck, these works made subsequent scholarship, including the conference from which this book is drawn, possible. We express our appreciation and respect to these filmmakers and authors.

During a long and distinguished career, Buck earned high praise for her pioneering work. Her friend and fellow best-selling author James Michener called Buck, "a spokesman on all sorts of issues: freedom of the press, freedom of religion, the adoptability of disadvantaged children, the future of China, especially the battle for women's rights, for education. If you followed in her trail, as I did, you were put in touch with almost every major movement in the

United States—intellectual, social, and political." Given the salience of the issues Buck wrote about and the urgency to (re)kindle interest in Buck's legacy, 2016 seemed an auspicious year for a conference focused on Buck.

The Pearl S. Buck "Living Gateway" Conference was held on the WVU campus in Morgantown, West Virginia, September 11–13, 2016. The title "Living Gateway" refers to a phrase Buck used to describe her birthplace in rural West Virginia. Many of the essays in this book were invited by the editors based on presentations delivered at the conference, with special attention to those that help place Buck in a global or transnational perspective. In a few cases, the editors invited submissions from members of the scholarly and creative communities with a particular interest or expertise in Buck but who were unable to attend the conference.

The book contains nine chapters, authored by scholars in disciplines ranging from American studies and history to English and creative writing. These chapters are loosely organized into three broad categories: foreign policy and global affairs (David M. Crowe, Donn Rogosin, and Charles Kupfer); new views on Asia (Junwei Yao, T. J. Park, and David Gordon); and interpretations of literary vision (Kang Liao, Carol Breslin, and Rob Merritt).

David Crowe, professor emeritus of history and law at Elon University, built his distinguished academic career with pathfinding research on war crimes, genocide, and the Holocaust. David Crowe's work on Raphael Lemkin, the man who coined the term "genocide," brought him into contact with Pearl Buck. An advocate of many humanitarian causes, Buck joined forces with Lemkin to help him win support for his major initiative—the establishment of the world's first Genocide Convention. In his essay, "Pearl Buck, Raphael Lemkin, and the Struggle for the Genocide Convention," Crowe shows how Buck's efforts and networks proved indispensable to Lemkin—helping him ultimately to succeed.

Donn Rogosin, an American studies scholar and independent documentary filmmaker from New York and cowriter and producer of the Buck documentary *East Wind, West Wind*, offers a blend of observation and analysis in his chapter, "Pearl Buck and the Evolution of American Foreign Policy: Reflections and Speculations of Her Film Biographer." Weaving together the warp of America's interactions with the world during the twentieth century with the woof of Buck's own life and global experiences, Rogosin produces a thought-provoking tapestry.

Charles Kupfer, professor of American studies at Penn State Harrisburg concentrates on a single speech delivered by Pearl Buck during World War II. In "Pearl Buck's Strategic Vision: Decolonization, Desegregation, and Second World War Imperatives," Kupfer explains how Pearl Buck's 1942 address at the Astor Hotel in New York laid out her remarkable vision for America's domestic and foreign policy during the war and its aftermath. Buck called for the creation of a postwar global order, one that would be led by the United States and that would be based on the American principles of democracy and equality. European colonialism, Buck insisted, must not play a role in the postwar geopolitical landscape. However, before America could speak with moral authority on the subject of Europe's treatment of nonwhite races, the country had to end its discriminatory treatment of minorities at home. In Kupfer's deft retelling of this pivotal speech, Buck comes across as an intellectual and humanitarian who was far ahead of her time and far ahead of the other luminaries of her day, none of whom discerned the subtle linkage of colonization abroad with segregation at home.

Junwei Yao, professor at Nanjing Normal University and authority on Pearl Buck, explains China's recent embrace of the writer from the perspective of a Chinese scholar. In "Chinese Culture 'Going Global': Pearl S. Buck's Methodological Inspiration," Yao reviews how Buck, in the twentieth century, used the novel to teach Americans about Chinese customs and traditions. To prove his point, Yao introduces readers to the key works by Buck that penetrate deep into the heart of Chinese culture. In the twenty-first century, her literary influence has started to attract the attention of Chinese government officials and scholars. Once dismissive of Buck, these groups increasingly recognize the power of her novels to promote Chinese culture overseas. Buck's novels, in sum, exist in happy alignment with China's "Going Global" initiative, intended to spread Chinese literature, culture, and values around the world.

Shifting geographic focus to Korea, T. J. Park, a professor of history at West Virginia State University, explores Buck's impact on perceptions and realities of Korean identity in his chapter, "Pearl S. Buck's Promising Legacy in South Korea: The Pearl S. Buck Foundation and the Rise of Korean Multiculturalism." Drawing on a variety of original sources, including personal correspondence and government documents, Park details Buck's lesser-known endeavors in Korea.

David Gordon, chair of the history department at Shepherd University, breaks new ground with his essay, "'Always in Love with Great Ends': Pearl S. Buck on Sun Yat-sen and His Nationalist Revolution." For decades, scholars have been mining Buck's writings to ascertain her views on China, its culture, its people, and its governments. They have overlooked, however, Buck's nuanced and shifting opinion on Sun Yat-sen, the founder of the Chinese Republic. Gordon rectifies this omission. In his essay, he introduces readers to the key writings in the vast Buck corpus in which Buck offers her personal commentary on the "father of modern China." The essay includes Gordon's fascinating analysis of two neglected, if not entirely forgotten, texts: a play entitled *Sun Yat-sen* (1944) and a children's book, *The Man Who Changed China: The Story of Sun Yat-sen* (1953).

Kang Liao, professor at the Middlebury Institute of International Studies at Monterey, credits Buck with being the first author to render accurate depictions of Chinese peasant life in the countryside. In his essay, "China's Recent Realization: The Real Peasant Life Portrayed by Pearl S. Buck," Liao tracks the trajectory of Buck's reputation in China as an authority on the Chinese countryside. Though popular in the West, Buck was largely dismissed in China after the Communist Revolution in 1949. Readers will find fascinating Liao's rich description and analysis of the Chinese novels set in the countryside, sanctioned by the Communist Party, which flourished in her absence. The essay also discusses the recent resurgence of interest in Buck, which has restored her literary reputation in China and convinced Chinese scholars to revisit her portrayal of the Chinese peasant.

Carol Breslin, a professor emerita of English at Gwynedd Mercy University in Pennsylvania and an affiliate of the Pearl S. Buck International, provides a literary analysis of Buck's most famous novel in her chapter, "Gateways into *The Good Earth*: Myth, Archetype, and Symbol in Pearl S. Buck's Classic Novel." Buck's style has often been characterized as straightforward and not very allegorical; Breslin's analysis opens up the book to new and deeper—indeed, more global—interpretations.

As a poet and professor of English at Bluefield College in Virginia, Rob Merritt approaches Buck as a fellow writer and suggests ways she can influence the creative process in his chapter, "'Not Having to Be Alone Is Happiness': The Cal Price Writing Workshops at the Pearl Buck Birthplace as Catalysts for a Glocal Writing Community." Merritt demonstrates how Buck, by bridging the global and local (glocal) in her own writing, shines the light on a similar path for other writers.

For decades, Pearl Buck scholarship has tended to focus on her Chinese experience and the influence her novels have had on teaching Westerners about China. However, researchers have recently begun to branch out—to explore new themes, new topics, and new directions relating to Buck. This volume of essays represents our attempt to showcase some of the new scholarship. If it is indicative of what is to come, this new direction in Pearl Buck studies promises to be as fertile as the China-centered research of past decades. If this volume helps to stimulate new scholarship about Buck in a global and interdisciplinary perspective, it will have exceeded our expectations.

CHAPTER 1

Pearl Buck, Raphael Lemkin, and the Struggle for the Genocide Convention

David M. Crowe

In 1947, Pearl S. Buck, one of the United States' most prominent authors and social activists, joined forces with Raphael Lemkin, a Polish-Jewish lawyer who had fled Poland in 1939 and later settled in the United States, to try to convince the new United Nations to adopt a convention that declared genocide a crime under international law. Unlike Buck, who had won Nobel and Pulitzer prizes for her literary works, Lemkin, who came to the United States in 1941, was relatively unknown until he published his book *Axis Rule in Occupied Europe* in late 1944. It quickly gained a wide audience, particularly chapter 9 of the book, which coined and defined the crime of genocide. Buck, who had written widely about Japanese crimes in China during the war, was quite aware of the genocidal nature of such crimes, so when Lemkin asked her in 1947 to draft a memo that he would use to convince UN members to adopt a Genocide Convention, she readily agreed. Over the next eighteen months, she personally contacted a number of prominent international figures about the importance of adopting the Genocide Convention, and wrote articles for newspapers in the United States and Europe about its importance. After its adoption in 1948, she nominated Lemkin for the Nobel Peace Prize, and later wrote that she was proud of all that she had done to help convince others of the importance of the convention's adoption. She did so, she added, not only because of the importance of the convention but also her deep respect for Lemkin.

At a distance, Buck and Lemkin would seem to have little in common, given the former's life in China and the latter's birth and early career in tsarist Russia and interwar Poland. Yet they shared a distant background that would partially play a role in the campaign they both helped wage to convince the United Nations to adopt the Genocide Convention in 1947–48. Both, in different ways, were refugees from war-torn East Asia and Eastern Europe. They were also gifted linguists and writers who were deeply committed to human rights in the broadest sense of the word. Buck left China in 1934 and Lemkin fled Poland seven years later in the face of the Nazi onslaught against that country, ultimately settling in the United States in 1941.

Lemkin, a lawyer by training, had long been concerned about the impact of modern industrialized war on various ethnic groups. In the fall of 1933, he presented a paper at an International Conference for the Unification of Criminal Law in Madrid that drew on earlier works by prominent international jurists such as Vespasian Pella who called for new international laws against "crimes of barbarity" and "crimes of vandalism" that could cause "a common danger." Lemkin's paper embraced Pella's ideas but also went further and discussed crimes that were both "attacks against individual human rights" that "relate to the relations between the individual and the collectivity." The most serious of such crimes, he went on, were "*acts of extermination* directed against the ethnic, religious or special collectivities whatever the motive (political, religious, etc.), for example massacres, pogroms, actions taken to ruin the economic existence of the members of the collectivity, etc. Also belonging in this category are all sorts of brutalities which attack the dignity of the individual in cases where these acts of humiliation have their source in a campaign of extermination directed against the collectivity in which the victim is a member."[1] Such acts, he added, were offenses "against the law of nations" that should be called "*barbarity.*"[2]

He went on to discuss acts of vandalism, which he described as the "systematic and organized destruction of the art and cultural heritage" of a collectivity that presented its "unique genius and achievement."[3] He then proposed legislation that, among other things, made it an "*offense of barbarity*" to commit "an action against the life, the bodily integrity, liberty, dignity or economic existence of a person belonging to such a collectivity (racial, religious, social)." He added that the "*offense of vandalism*" also be considered a crime if it resulted in the destruction of "works of cultural or artistic heritage."[4] Though little came of these ideas at the time, they provided Lemkin with the nucleus of his later writings on war crimes and genocide.

Buck, of course, was keenly aware that such crimes had been committed by the Japanese in China during the long conflict there from 1931 to 1945, though there is no indication that she was aware of Lemkin's ideas. In late January 1932, for example, the Japanese military initiated "the world's first air raid on an unprotected civilian target the size of Shanghai, setting the precedent for Guernica and the Second World War."[5] This was followed five years later by the formal Japanese invasion of China, which triggered the War of Resistance or Sino-Japanese War, a conflict that still haunts Chinese-Japanese relations. Though estimates vary, approximately fourteen to sixteen million Chinese died in this conflict,[6] while thousands of others suffered from unspeakable Japanese crimes and atrocities. The mass rape of Chinese women in Nanjing in late 1937 and early 1938 was only the "tip of the iceberg," so to speak, of such crimes. The mass execution of civilians was commonplace, while tens of thousands of Chinese women were forced to become "comfort women" for the Japanese military.[7] One Nationalist official, Chuang-Ying Hsu, was stunned by the "action(s) of Japanese soldiers towards women," something "we can never dream of in [*sic*] this civilized world. The Japanese soldiers—they are so fond of raping—so fond of women, and that one cannot believe."[8] The Japanese also conducted cruel human biological experiments on captives and used chemical weapons during the war. In the fall of 1940, for example, Japanese planes dropped wheat that contained "plague-infected fleas" on the city of Ningbo in southern China.[9]

Pearl Buck wrote Eleanor Roosevelt in the summer of 1940 about what she called Japan's unspeakable "barbaric invasion" of China. She hoped that Mrs. Roosevelt would consider contributing to the Women's Committee of Tribute to China to help send medical supplies to save "the lives of thousands of Chinese woman and children." Those who contributed to the fund would have their names inscribed in a Book of Hope, whose introduction spoke about the need to protect the "dignity and rights of human personality" that was threatened by the "destructive force" of "despotism in the world."[10]

She also addressed these crimes in several of the novels she wrote about China during the war. The first, *The Patriot* (1939), deals with the life of I-wan, the son of a wealthy Shanghai banker, and his involvement in the major upheavals that swept China in the 1920s and 1930s.[11] She ends her second, and perhaps most poignant wartime novel, *Dragon Seed: The Story of China at War* (1941), with Lao Er, the son of the novel's principal character, Ling Tan, answering his father's question about whether there was a promise of rain: "Only a promise,'" Lao Er responded.[12] She then begins the third book, *The Promise,* by writing that "in their despair men must hope, when a promise is given, though it is only a promise.[13] *The Promise* (1942, 1943), deals with Chiang Kai-shek's failed efforts working with the British in wartime Burma.

Though only a novel, *Dragon Seed* describes in shocking detail Japan's cruel treatment of the Chinese people during the War of Resistance. Over time, the Japanese found themselves bogged down in a war of attrition and by 1941 only controlled the important eastern parts of the country. The Japanese set up a collaborationist government (the Government of National Salvation) under Wang Jingwei, a former ally of Chiang Kai-shek, in Nanjing (the old Nationalist capital), which called itself the Republic of China. Bold Chinese resistance (both Nationalist and Communist) played an important role in limiting Japan's efforts to conquer all of China and ultimately helped defeat the Japanese.[14]

Dragon Seed begins months after Japan invaded China after the Marco Polo bridge incident outside of Beijing in early July 1937. After quickly taking Beijing, the Japanese moved southward, taking Shanghai after a three-month campaign against Chiang Kai-shek's forces. They then moved westward to take Nanjing.[15] It is at this point that a peddler tells Ling Tan, the principal character in *Dragon Seed*, that the "East-Ocean dwarfs" (the Japanese) had "killed men, women and children" in the north.[16] This is a hint of what is to come, though in the early chapters of *Dragon Seed* Buck deals principally with the bucolic simplicity of the life of Ling Tan's family.[17]

This soon changed as Japanese troops entered their village en route to Nanjing. At first, the villagers were only concerned about the "flying ships" that were bombing nearby Nanjing. Next came a flood of refugees, followed by the Japanese. Before they arrived, Ling Tan called the villagers together and they agreed that, being a "defenseless" village, they should greet the conquerors "courteously."[18] Heartened by Japanese leaflets that promised villagers that they had nothing to fear from their troops, their hope soon turned to horror after they watched Japanese soldiers attack village elders with their bayonets. More shocking was the mass rape of an elderly woman, a crime repeatedly discussed in the novel. Ling Sao, Ling Tan's wife, soon discovered, after listening to the stories of many of the female refugees, that the savage, brutal rape of Chinese women was commonplace in any area under Japanese control.[19] Soon, these distant crimes reached the village. After occupying it, the Japanese demanded that all of the female refugees who had fled to Tan's house had to come with them, or suffer the consequences. After a lot of fearful soul searching, the refugee women went with the Japanese troops and became "comfort women" who were continually raped by Japanese soldiers.[20] Ling Tan's family soon fell victim to these crimes after his daughter-in-law, Orchid, innocently ventured into Nanjing, where she was gang-raped and strangled to death by five Japanese soldiers.[21]

As conditions worsened, Ling Er, one of Ling Tan's sons, convinced the villagers to do what they could to resist the Japanese. This included refusing to grow certain crops and storing weapons for Chinese guerillas in the nearby hills. The book ends in 1941 with Ling Tang and his family crushed by the weight of Japanese rule. All that remained, in terms of hope, was "Only a promise."[22]

Dragon Seed provided American readers with a graphic picture of the crimes committed by the Japanese in China. The "Rape of Nanjing" had been fully covered by the press in 1937–38, and came to symbolize the cruelty of the Japanese occupation. It also stirred a deep hatred of the Japanese that was further inflamed after Pearl Harbor. Although rape is an eternal crime of war, it took on new meaning in World War II because it was used in Asia and Europe to deeply humiliate an enemy. It is estimated, for example, that Soviet troops raped as many as two million German women after they entered Reich territory in early 1945.[23]

The Germans committed equally ghastly crimes throughout Europe. The worst of these was the mass murder of six million Jews in ghettos, concentration camps, and death camps. It was stories of these crimes that motivated Lemkin to move beyond the ideas he proposed in 1933 and later call for a more robust body of war crimes law that would be enshrined in international legislation designed to outlaw them. Part of what motivated him was the rise of Nazism and Hitler's adoption of stringent anti-Semitic laws and decrees that gradually stripped Reich Jews of their most basic rights and freedoms. Yet any distant concerns Lemkin had about what was taking place in Germany became deeply personal after Hitler invaded Poland in the fall of 1939. Lemkin, who fled to Sweden weeks after the invasion, left his parents and a large extended family behind, most of whom were murdered by the Nazis in Treblinka or Auschwitz.[24]

Lemkin spent a year in Sweden where he collected documents on German occupation policies in Europe. In early 1941, he was invited to teach at Duke University's law school and later moved to Washington where he worked as a consultant for the Board of Economic Warfare and the Foreign Economic Administration. In June 1944, he tried to get a position with the Office of Foreign Economic Administration as a consultant on continental law.[25]

Later that year, he published his seminal work, *Axis Rule in Occupied Europe: Laws of Occupation, Analysis of Government, Proposals for Redress*. For the most part, *Axis Rule* is Lemkin's analysis of the large collection of documents that he had been gathering on Nazi and Italian occupation policies in Europe. Part 1, "German Techniques of Occupation," looks at the German administration in occupied areas, and the Nazi use of police, law, and the courts to seize or control property, finance, and labor.[26] Chapter 8, "The Legal Status of Jews," briefly discusses their "special status" throughout Nazi-occupied Europe, followed by chapter 9, "Genocide." The second part of his study, "The Occupied Countries," deals specifically with general German and Italian occupation policies in various countries throughout Europe, while part 3 covers the specifics of occupation in each of these countries.

For the most part, *Axis Rule* is usually read and studied only in the context of Lemkin's brief chapter 9 on genocide. In part 1, "Genocide—A New Term and New Conception for Destruction of Nations," he defines genocide as "the destruction of a national or ethnic group." He then discusses the two phases of genocide, explaining that they involve the "destruction of the national pattern of the oppressed group," and the "imposition of the national pattern of the oppressor."[27] And though he thinks that such practices were normally described as "denationalization," he argues that this interpretation often was used simply to describe the "deprivation of citizenship." He also considers it inadequate because it did not "connote the destruction of the biological structure," or the "imposition of the national pattern of the oppressor." Genocide, he explains, was the "antithesis" of the Rousseau-Portalis Doctrine, which was "implicit in the Hague Regulations," particularly Hague IV (1907). According to this doctrine, war was aimed against "sovereigns and armies, not against subjects and civilians." According to Lemkin, the current war in Europe was not just against "states and their armies, but against peoples." Hitler's concept of genocide, he adds, was based on "biological patterns," not cultural ones. Some groups such as the Jews were "to be destroyed completely."[28]

In part 2 Lemkin discusses the eight "techniques" of genocide—political, social, cultural, economic, biological, physical, religious, and moral—and provides specific examples from various countries occupied by the Nazis, particularly Poland, to underscore the effectiveness of such "techniques." He is extremely sensitive to Nazi policies against Jews and Christian Poles, particularly with cultural, religious, and economic issues. The Nazis, he adds, used biological and physical methods to depopulate and annihilate certain groups throughout Europe, particularly through forced malnutrition. They also practiced systematic religious persecution to destroy the idea of "religious leadership."[29]

In part 3 Lemkin proposes that with the end of the war in sight, amendments should be made to the "Hague Regulations [Hague IV, 1907[30]] expressly to prohibit genocide in any war which may occur in the future." Such amendments, he argues, must "consist of two essential parts: in the first should be included every action infringing upon the life, liberty, health, corporal integrity, economic existence, and the honor of the inhabitants when committed because they belong to a national, religious, or racial group; and in the second, every policy aiming at the destruction of the aggrandizement of one of such groups to the prejudice or detriment of another."[31] He adds that genocide was not just a problem "of war but also of peace," particularly in Europe, where minorities were continually being persecuted, both at home and abroad. He advocates the creation of an "international multilateral treaty" that would provide strong legal protections for minority groups in each country. The signatory powers of such a treaty would also agree to include such provisions not only in their constitutions and criminal laws but also "penalties for genocide practices."[32]

Lemkin's book created a bit of a stir in the United States because it came out just as Washington was giving serious consideration to the creation of a special tribunal to try German war criminals. Though the major powers had warned Germany and Japan's leaders that they would be held legally accountable for war crimes committed by their troops, with the exception of the work of the United Nations War Crime Commission, little attention was given to this matter until it became apparent in the fall of 1944 that Germany would soon be defeated. The question of trying major German war criminals was closely linked to concerns about the nature of the Allied occupation of Germany once the European war was over. One of the first major proposals about the occupation was drawn up by Henry Morgenthau, Franklin Delano Roosevelt's secretary of the treasury, in response to a State Department memo that argued for maintaining German unity and rebuilding German industry to ensure a "minimum standard of living" for the German people and enhance Germany's ability to pay reparations and restitution. Instead, Morgenthau proposed that postwar Germany be transformed "into a primarily pastoral community" too weak to threaten Europe and the world."[33]

This idea was actively supported by the Society for the Prevention of World War III (SPWW3), which was made up of prominent, influential public figures in the United States. In the fall of 1944, the SPWW3 initiated a major campaign to convince the American public and US leaders to adopt Morgenthau's plan. One of these figures was Pearl Buck, who was a member of the organization's advisory board. In this role, she was asked to do everything possible to convince the US government to adopt stringent policies toward postwar Germany. As part of its national campaign, the SPWW3 also urged "commentators like Walter Winchell to 'popularize' the word 'genocide' to describe Nazi crimes." It also urged the release of documents that confirmed "the Nazis' unprecedented 'campaign of terror and brutality.'"[34]

Pearl Buck saw all of this from a different perspective. A passionate advocate for civil and human rights in the United States, she saw international plans at the end of World War II, particularly what she considered "imperialistic" efforts to restore lost colonial empires, as a "return to the racial status quo," which, if allowed to go forward, could cause World War III. She warned that if these colonial empires were restored then it would lead countries in Asia to turn "to Russia for leadership in the postwar struggle."[35]

At the time, Lemkin was involved in discussions about the creation of a tribunal to try Germany's major war criminals. He wrote Supreme Court Justice Robert Jackson soon after President Harry Truman appointed him chief US prosecutor for what would become the Nuremberg International Military Tribunal (1945–46), and suggested he read *Axis Rule* and a recent article he had written about genocide since they provided "some legal evidence as to war crimes."[36] Lemkin was soon hired by the Pentagon's War Crimes Office as a consultant for a prosecutorial "control squad" that would work on a sample trial brief. When this did not work out, Lemkin was chosen to work with Telford Taylor, one of Jackson's top assistants, for "encyclopedic purposes in the War Crimes office."[37]

Lemkin, unfortunately, gained a reputation for being difficult to work with. In fairness, part of the reason was that he was plagued by nightmares and worries about the fate of his parents. He was also troubled by questions about the thoroughness of his research for *Axis Rule*. Regardless, he was ultimately sent to London where he was asked to work with the head of the Soviet delegation, Gen. I. T. Nikitchenko, and other organizations to gather further evidence on German atrocities in Poland.[38]

Lemkin, who was aggressively promoting his ideas about genocide, did everything he could to convince the prosecution to adopt genocide as one of the charges in the Nuremberg indictment. Though his idea was rejected, it was included in Count Three, War Crimes, Section A, "Murder and Ill-Treatment of Civilian Populations." The term was also mentioned during the trial by some of the prosecutors.[39] Lemkin hoped this would help convince the judges to cite the term in their judgment, which they did not, even though the crimes they described in that section of the indictment dealing with the ill treatment of civilians certainly fit the definition of genocide: "In Poland and the Soviet Union these crimes were part of a plan to get rid of whole native populations by expulsion and annihilation."[40] Disappointed, Lemkin was extremely critical of the outcome of the trial, calling it "wholly insufficient."[41]

Frustrated, he now turned his energies to the new United Nations, which was meeting at Lake Success in Long Island. He mounted a campaign to convince UN delegates to adopt a resolution that would recognize that genocide was a crime in international law, and he asked member states to begin the process of preparing a draft convention for consideration by the General Assembly. After considerable discussion in the UN's Sixth (Legal) Committee,[42] the General Assembly adopted two interrelated resolutions on December 11, 1946. Resolution 95(1) asked the Committee on the Codification of International Law (later the International Law Commission) to formulate "in the context of a general codification of offences against the peace and security of mankind, or of an International Criminal Code, of the principles recognized in the Charter of the Nürnberg Tribunal and in the judgment of the Tribunal." Resolution 96(1) affirmed that genocide was "a crime under international law" that was "punishable." It requested that the Economic and Social Council (ECOSOC) study the prospect of preparing a draft convention on genocide that "would be submitted to the next regular session of the General Assembly."[43]

In the spring of 1947, Lemkin was appointed to a committee of three prominent international lawyers (Vespasian Pella and Henri Donnedieu de Vabres were the other members) to prepare a draft

Genocide Convention. Unfortunately, there were serious disagreements among Lemkin, Pella, and de Vabres about what should be covered in the draft, so they sent ECOSOC a wide range of options for a possible convention.[44] Consequently, ECOSOC decided to ask the UN's executive branch, the secretariat, headed by Secretary-General Trygve Lie, to prepare a draft of the convention.[45] It completed a new draft and submitted it to all UN member nations for further comment.[46] Lemkin, now concerned about possible delays in the submission of a draft to the General Assembly, decided to give up his position with the War Department and move to New York, where he could mount a public campaign to ensure its adoption in a timely manner.[47]

One of the first people he turned to for help was Pearl Buck. At this point, it is difficult to gauge how well they knew each other. *The New York Times* and the *New York Post* had published numerous articles and editorials on *Axis Rule* and Lemkin's efforts at Nuremberg and the United Nations, so she was well aware of his work.[48] He only mentioned her once in his autobiography, but in a way that indicated they had been working together for some time.[49] Lemkin also wrote that in "1945 and in subsequent years the contributions of individual women and of women's organizations to the issue of genocide was considerable. . . . Unknowingly, they are the creators of moral philosophy for the benefit of every human being."[50] This would certainly apply to Buck, whom one of her admirers wrote was an "ambassador-extraordinary for the cause of world peace and international understanding.[51]

Buck was extremely proud of her work with Lemkin, and Harris wrote in his biography of her that it was an example of her "interest in civil rights" that "held to the principle of equality for all."[52] Lemkin first approached her in the summer of 1947 about writing a draft "manifesto" that could be used to convince UN members of the urgency of adopting the convention. The manifesto that she wrote stressed the urgency of a Genocide Convention, given the "recent genocide in Germany." This was merely an example of similar crimes in history, she went on, while the "weak, the helpless, the innocent, wherever they are, live in continuing fear. The strong, the ruthless, the arrogant, can continue also, unless and until the principles of human decency are transferred into international attitudes, statements, and laws, providing for the effective protection of the weak, the innocent, and the helpless against the strong and the ruthless." She added that "Life in our world is enriched by the diversity of cultures and ideas which proceed from variety in racial, national, and religious groups, even as a community is the better for variety in its citizens. The destruction of variety would be an intolerable loss to mankind, and there is no guarantee, moreover, that the surviving groups or group would be the best ones." "Homicide," she went on, is recognized throughout the world a punishable crime," while genocide is "still allowed, condoned, and sometimes rewarded." Yet in many ways, she added,

> genocide is a threat greater than war, for it is perpetuated in peace as well as war, it is contagious, spreading from one community to another, catching at fanatic fringes of the population and spreading like forest fire, through fear. Indeed, in the last war the victims of genocide were greater than the victims of war.
>
> It was now imperative for the global community to adopt a manifesto to remind mankind that human groups have the right to live in liberty and peace in accordance with other human individuals. Such free human groups, united by ethnical, religious, and cultural ties, are a great living force in civilization. The concept of the prevention of genocide envisages human groups in their organic entirety including physical existence, biological continuity, and the basic elements of spiritual life. The protection of the spirit is as important as the protection of the body.

The manifesto went on to say that the United Nation's adoption of this "great and constructive principle" would reassure a world "divided by wars, misunderstandings, and uncertainties." It is the "right of all human beings to live safely within the groups to which they have been born and to which they spiritually belong, and that the violation of this right, which is genocide, shall be held an international crime."[53]

Once the manifesto was completed, Lemkin asked Buck to "communicate with various world leaders" and ask them to support his efforts at the United Nations. What followed was a flurry of letters and wires from Buck to prominent international figures urgently asking them to sign the manifesto, which would be presented before the UN General Assembly with Lemkin's proposal for official recognition of genocide as a crime.

On September 3, 1947, Buck, along with Lemkin and François Mauriac, who was awarded the Nobel Prize in Literature in 1952, sent wires to Count Folke Bernadotte, the vice president of the Swedish Red Cross who played a key role in the liberation of prisoners in several concentration camps;[54] Princess Julianna of The Netherlands (who became queen a year later); Paal Berg, the former chief justice of the Norwegian Supreme Court; the Norwegian writer Sigrid Undset, who was awarded the Nobel Prize in Literature in 1928; Gabriela Mistrala (Lucila Godoy y Alcayaga), the Chilean poet who received it in 1945; and Refling Hagen, a prominent Norwegian writer, asking that they send letters of support for the manifesto to the General Assembly.[55]

While these letters did help garner international support for the manifesto, it faced opposition from Great Britain and the Soviet Union. In meetings of the Legal Committee (LC) from October 1–6, Sir Hartley Shawcross, the British prosecutor at the Nuremberg trial, said that while he supported the idea that biological genocide was a crime, the convention went beyond this concept, thus creating "an entirely new body of international law." If it was approved as written, he argued, "it would do more harm than good." After considerable discussion, the LC voted to send it to Subcommittee 2 "to examine the procedure to be followed in considering the question of genocide."[56]

Initially, Lemkin and others saw this move as a tactic to delay action on the manifesto.[57] But nine days later, Buck wrote Dr. Ricardo J. Alfaro, the Panamanian chair of the LC, praising the move and suggesting that the chair of the subcommittee be from China, a country that had a "high and fine record in regard to the treatment of human groups." The letter, obviously written in consultation with Lemkin, then made a series of suggestions about changes in several of the articles. She added that people throughout the world, but particularly in the United States, "watch the work of the United Nations and long for great constructive measures." She apologized for not meeting Dr. Alfaro personally to discuss all of this, but said she would be more than happy to meet him at his office. She also invited him for tea with her and her husband at their New York apartment. Dr. Alfaro wrote back that he would do everything he could "to secure prompt and thorough consideration of the draft convention."[58]

The new chair of the subcommittee was Tsiang Tingfu (Jiang Tingfu), the newly appointed Chinese ambassador to the United Nations. Buck had written him in mid-October seeking his support of Lemkin's efforts to get the General Assembly to approve the genocide proposal. Tsiang thanked her for the letter and noted that "China has been in the vanguard of those who desire to see at all costs, a really living convention of genocide put into effect." But he reminded her that even though genocide was "recognized and repudiated by all decent minded people," its "prevention and punishment call for [a] careful and detailed definition of the crime" so "that nations or groups who would seek its perpetration, can find no legal loophole by which to justify their acts." He also told her that he had been asked to chair Subcommittee 2, apparently unaware that she had nominated him for the position.[59]

On November 21, the General Assembly approved two resolutions (one from China) that asked ECOSOC to continue its work on "the suppression of the crime of genocide, including the study of the draft convention prepared by the Secretariat," and to report its progress at the next session of the General Assembly.[60]

A few weeks later, Lemkin asked Buck to send a new letter to twenty-two prominent intellectuals, writers, politicians, jurists, and academics, and share with them news about the United Nations' decision. She wrote them that there were delegates who opposed the convention and, despite widespread support for it, "the battle is not yet won" since the secretariat's draft convention was still being reviewed by UN member states. Buck also asked them to request their governments to urge the secretary general to expedite the "drafting of a final convention." She included a copy of the resolution passed by Panama's legislature supporting the convention, and included further information about the question of genocide "in the hope that you might find it possible to utilize it for arousing public interest in the subject."[61]

Lemkin approached Buck again in early 1948 and asked her to write an article for newspapers in Scandinavia and the United Kingdom about the convention. She responded that she had just sent letters to the editors of the Danish newspaper *Politiken* and the *Manchester Guardian*. In her "Letter to Denmark," she said that when she lived in China she had always viewed Denmark as "a country of pleasant memory and of warm hope." Her later visits there, she added, confirmed her sense that Denmark was a country of "humane common sense." She was saddened when war swept through Denmark but was heartened by the brave Danish effort to save its Jews, the act of a nation that had always been "a leader in humanitarian affairs." Consequently, she was pleased that Denmark was a member of the UN's ECOSOC committee. She then defined genocide and explained why it should be considered an international crime. She was concerned, though, about legalistic criticism of the draft convention by some UN members. And while she thought that some of these concerns might have merit, she was fearful that such criticism might lead to delays in its adoption. She also noted comments by Finn Seyersted, a member of Norway's UN delegation, "that the Nuremberg Principles have to do with war," while "genocide is a danger even in times of peace."[62]

For centuries, Buck went on, genocidal acts were always considered "affairs private to the nation," meaning those who committed them were "not considered criminals." Consequently, justice was often meted out via acts of revenge such as the murder of Enver Pasha, the Turkish leader responsible for the deaths of "hundreds of thousands of Armenians" during World War I. Such "single-handed justice is anarchical," she argued, and now was the time to declare that individuals or groups who "commit genocide are guilty of [an] international crime." She appealed to the people of Denmark to support efforts in the United Nations to adopt a Genocide Convention to ensure that the world was "safe for peoples of all creeds, races, nations, and cultures."[63]

Her more extensive letter to the *Manchester Guardian* heaped praise on the British for their sense of humanity and civilization, and said this was reflected in the fact that the head of the UK's delegation to the United Nations, Sir Hartley Shawcross, took the lead in December 1946 to get the General Assembly to adopt Lemkin's genocide resolution. She reminded British readers not only of the genocide of the Jews during the Holocaust, but also the genocidal murder of thousands of Haitians in the Dominican Republic in the 1930s. Such crimes, whether during times of war or peace, were threats to "humanity as a whole." A "law against genocide," Buck wrote, would have prevented Joachim von Ribbentrop from serving as German ambassador to the United Kingdom while his country was persecuting Jews. The same was true for the crimes of Enver Pasha, who walked the street of Tiflis (Tblisi), Georgia, as a free man before his assassination. She also restated Seyersted's comments about mixing the laws of war with the laws of peace," and added that "a world full of distress and anxiety cannot wait for security until lawyers have made up their minds about large codifications of international law." From Buck's perspective, the nature of genocidal crimes, which took place during times of peace and war, demanded immediate attention and could not await the glacial deliberations of lawyers and others.

She also pointed out the broad international support for the convention. She noted, for example, that there was a large body of UN material in the United Kingdom on the history of the Genocide Convention for those who wanted to know more about it, as well as Lemkin's two principal works on the whole question of genocide—his 1946 article in *American Scholar* and *Axis Rule in Occupied Europe*. She ended by reminding readers of all that had been done by the British to alleviate the suffering of Christians during the Ottoman era, and hoped that once again the United Kingdom would lead the way "in this new humanitarian intervention, to prevent and punish genocide."[64] Buck sent copies of these letters to Lemkin, who thanked her for them but mildly chided her for the way she used the word "genocide." Apologetically, she wrote that she could "quite see that it should not be confused with mass murder."[65]

Buck also spent a lot of time in the spring of 1948 corresponding with diplomats and politicians she knew to garner support for the convention.[66] In March, the ECOSOC's Social Committee appointed an *ad hoc* committee made up of representatives from China, France, Lebanon, Poland, the United States, the USSR, and Venezuela to prepare a draft of the convention.[67] Chaired by John Matkos, the US representative on the committee, it spent five weeks in April and May preparing a draft. Some of the early disagreements centered around the inclusion of political groups as possible victims of genocide and the question of cultural genocide. There were also questions about jurisdiction, and whether an international court should be created to handle such cases, or a criminal chamber of the International Court of Justice, which had been created in 1945. On April 28, the committee adopted a nine-article draft convention that included political groups, cultural genocide, and the jurisdiction of national courts or a "competent international tribunal."[68]

Several days earlier, the new Committee for an International Genocide Convention had its first meeting in New York and asked Buck to join its campaign to garner further support for the convention. In late July, Lemkin learned that the ECOSOC would be meeting in Geneva in August to discuss the *ad hoc* committee's draft. Worried about opposition from the British and the Soviets, and American opposition to the idea of cultural genocide, he flew to Geneva to do what he could to influence delegates about these issues.[69]

What he discovered was an intense British campaign to scuttle the convention. In a letter to Buck on September 7, he wrote that the British had tried to entice the American delegation to support placing the draft last on the ECOSOC's agenda so that there would be little time to discuss it fully. At the same time, the British proposed that the convention be "divided in two parts." The first would deal with physical genocide, which would be dealt with in connection with the codification of the Nuremberg Principles by the new International Law Commission (created by the UN to study the codification of international law). The second part would have the Human Rights Commission (which was preparing a Declaration on Human Rights) deal with the issue of cultural genocide which, Lemkin wrote, "does not deal with group rights at all." In the end, he concluded, "the British won the Geneva fight."[70]

At its August 26 meeting, ECOSOC decided, in light of these differences, that it would send the draft convention and the minutes of its meetings to the General Assembly for further action when it met in Paris in September.[71] Despite all of this, Lemkin concluded in his letter to Buck that "there are good chances to have the convention [discussion] in Paris," although it was now important to do everything possible to "win the support" of as many delegates as possible. He concluded that "we have both decided to have a genocide convention and I hope we will have it in Paris with the help of noble friends."[72]

On September 24, the General Assembly asked the Legal Committee to study and report on the draft of the ECOSOC. What followed over the next two months were extremely intense meetings and discussions about the Genocide Convention. It still faced strong opposition from the British and at times the Soviets. The most intense discussions centered on article 2, which dealt with the groups that would be considered victims of genocidal acts. In meetings from October 7 through October 23, the committee decided to eliminate political groups and cultural genocide from the draft.[73] Lemkin was extremely disappointed in the deletion of the latter and wrote that it left him with a "heavy heart." But he was afraid to wage a new battle over this issue because it might "endanger the passage of the convention."[74]

On November 13, the Legal Committee appointed a subcommittee to prepare a final draft, which it completed ten days later. The LC sent the final draft to the General Assembly on December 3, and after several days of discussion voted unanimously on December 9, 1948, to adopt *the Convention on the Prevention and Punishment of the Crime of Genocide.*[75] Lemkin, who was present during the voting, was numbed by the outcome. It, for him, meant a "new partnership between two worlds: my own world of long, frustrating efforts, hopes, and agonizing fears, and this new official world which now made a solemn pledge to preserve the life of the peoples and races of mankind."[76]

Yet he also knew that this was only one phase of the struggle for the convention—next came herculean efforts to get individual states to ratify it. This was completed a little over a year after it was adopted, and on January 12, 1951, the convention came into force. Lemkin, who died in 1959, worked hard to convince the US Senate to ratify it, which it finally did on November 4, 1988.[77]

Pearl Buck was extremely pleased with the convention's adoption and ratification, and she played a role in nominating Lemkin for the Nobel Peace Prize in 1950. Lemkin thanked her for the nomination, and she wrote back that she was extremely pleased to do so. She was asked again to consider nominating Lemkin in 1958 (he was nominated for the Peace Prize in 1950, 1951, 1955, 1956, 1958, and 1959). She wrote him that she did not know when she nominated him for the 1950 prize that is was "impermissible for such winners [she won the Nobel Prize in Literature in 1938] to nominate persons from other fields."[78] She told US Representative Emmanuel Celler, who initiated the 1958 nomination, that she knew "Professor Lemkin and think very highly of him and his work." In the end, Buck added, she "never regretted" the role she had played in supporting his efforts to get the United Nations to adopt the Genocide Convention.[79]

NOTES

1. Raphael Lemkin, "Acts Constituting a General (Transnational) Danger Considered as Offences against the Law of Nations," 4. http://www.preventgenocide.org/lemkin/madrid1933-english.htm (accessed August 31, 2016).
2. Ibid., 4.
3. Ibid., 5.
4. Ibid., 6–7.
5. David M. Crowe, *War Crimes, Genocide, and Justice: A Global History* (New York: Palgrave Macmillan, 2014), 126.
6. Rana Mitter estimates that 14 million Chinese died during the conflict. *Forgotten Ally: China's World War II, 1937–1945* (Boston: Houghton Mifflin Harcourt, 2013), 5, while R. J. Rummell's more outdated study puts Chinese losses at 3.4 to 16.9 million. *China's Bloody Century: Genocide and Mass Murder since 1900* (Brunswick, NJ: Transaction, 2007), 112, 132.
7. Crowe, *War Crimes*, 130–31.
8. Ibid., 129.
9. Ibid., 134–35.
10. Pearl S. Buck to Eleanor Roosevelt, June 12, 1940, Eleanor Roosevelt Papers, FDR Library, Hyde Park, NY, ER 709.
11. Pearl S. Buck, *The Patriot* (New York: John Day, 1939).
12. Buck, *Dragon Seed* (Kingston, RI: Moyer Bell, 2006), 378.
13. Pearl S. Buck, *The Promise* (New York: John Day, 1942, 1943), 1.
14. Crowe, *War Crimes*, 265–66.
15. Ibid., 128–29.

16. Buck, *Dragon Seed*, 8.
17. Ibid., 1–65.
18. Ibid., 66–86, 118–19.
19. Ibid., 123, 130, 146–47.
20. Ibid., 150–51.
21. Ibid., 178–81.
22. Ibid., 219, 223, 371–78.
23. Anthony Beevor, *The Fall of Berlin* (New York: Viking, 2002), 410.
24. Crowe, *War Crimes*, 285.
25. Raphael Lemkin, *Totally Unofficial: The Autobiography of Raphael Lemkin*, ed. Donna-Lee Frieze (New Haven, CT: Yale University Press, 2013), 112; Douglas B. Maggs to Oscar Cox, June 17, 1944, 1. Papers of Oscar S. Cox, FDR Library, Hyde Park, NY, Box 19.
26. Raphael Lemkin, *Axis Rule in Occupied Europe: Laws of Occupation, Analysis of Government, Proposals for Redress*, 2nd ed. (Clark, NJ: Law Book Exchange, 2008), 7–98.
27. Ibid., 79.
28. Ibid., 79–81. The 1907 *Convention Respecting the Laws and Customs of War on Land* was meant "to serve as a general rule of conduct for belligerents in their mutual relations and in their relations with the inhabitants." Carnegie Endowment for International Peace, *The Proceedings of the Hague Peace Conferences (1907)* (New York: Oxford University Press, 1920), 626.
29. Lemkin, *Axis Rule*, 82–90.
30. David M. Crowe, *War Crimes, Genocide, and Justice: A Global History* (New York: Palgrave Macmillan, 2014), 91–92.
31. Lemkin, *Axis Rule*, 93.
32. Ibid.
33. United States Department of State, *Foreign Relations of the United States Diplomatic Papers,* 1944, General, vol. 1 (Washington, DC: US Government Printing Office, 1944), 284, 285–87, 288, 291, 295; Crowe, *War Crimes*, 154.
34. Steven Casey, "The Campaign to Sell a Harsh Peace for Germany to the American Public, 1944–1948," *History* 90, no. 297 (2005): 2, 21, 27. Though President Roosevelt was initially sympathetic to the Morgenthau plan, Harry Truman, who succeeded him as president in the spring of 1945, strongly opposed it. This, coupled with the realities of the occupation of Germany and the Cold War, ultimately destroyed any thoughts of a harsh peace.
35. Peter Conn, *Pearl S. Buck: A Cultural Biography* (Cambridge: Cambridge University Press, 1996), 290–91.
36. John Q. Barrett, "Raphael Lemkin and 'Genocide' at Nuremberg, 1945–1946," in *The Genocide Convention Sixty Years after Its Adoption*, ed. Christoph Safferling and Eckart Conze (The Hague: T. M. C. Aser Press, 2010), 36.

37. Ibid., 39–41.
38. Lemkin, *Totally Unofficial*, 117; Barrett, "Raphael Lemkin," 42–45.
39. Office of United States Chief of Counsel for Prosecution of Axis Criminality, *Nazi Conspiracy and Aggression*, vol. 1 (Washington, DC: US Government Printing Office, 1946), 31–32; Barrett, "Raphael Lemkin," 47–48; Lemkin, *Totally Unofficial*, 118–20.
40. Office of United States Chief of Counsel for Prosecution of Axis Criminality, *Nazi Conspiracy and Aggression: Opinion and Judgment* (Washington, DC: US Government Printing Office, 1947), 66.
41. Lemkin, *Totally Unofficial*, 118.
42. The minutes of these meetings can be found in *The Genocide Convention: The Travaux Préparatories*, vol. 1, ed. Hirad Abthai and Philippa Webb (Leiden: Martinus Nijhoff, 2008), 3–34.
43. United Nations General Assembly, Resolution 95(1), Dec. 11, 1946, 188–89. www.un.org/documents/ga/res/1/ares1.htm (accessed September 7, 2016).
44. *Genocide Convention*, 67–114.
45. John Cooper, *Raphael Lemkin and the Struggle for the Genocide Convention* (Houndsmills: Palgrave Macmillan, 2008), 89.
46. *Genocide Convention*, 412–13.
47. Cooper, *Raphael Lemkin*, 88.
48. Barrett, "Raphael Lemkin," 49–50; Cooper, *Raphael Lemkin*, 45,61, 80–81.
49. Lemkin, *Totally Unofficial*, 136.
50. Ibid., 125.
51. Neil M. Barnett to Pearl S. Buck, May 18, 1942. Eleanor Roosevelt Papers, FDR Library, Hyde Park, NY, Box 1633.
52. Theodore F. Harris, in consultation with Pearl S. Buck, *Pearl S. Buck: A Biography*, vol. 2, *Her Philosophy as Expressed in Her Letters* (New York: John Day, 1971), 83.
53. Ibid., 84–85.
54. David M. Crowe, *The Holocaust: Roots, History, and Aftermath* (Boulder: Westview Press, 2008), 349–51.
55. François Mauriac, Pearl Buck, and Raphael Lemkin to Count Folke Bernadotte, Princess Juliana, Paal Berg, Sigrid Undset, Gabriela Mistral, and Refling Hagen, September 3, 1947. Raphael Lemkin Papers, Center for Jewish History (CJH), New York, Box 1, Folder 18, pp. 1–3.
56. *Genocide Convention*, 403–6.
57. Cooper, *Raphael Lemkin*, 100–101.
58. Harris, *Pearl S. Buck*, 86–87, 88.
59. Tsiang Tingfu to Pearl S. Buck, November 21, 1947, Raphael Lemkin Papers, CJH, Box 1, Folder 18, p. 1.
60. *Genocide Convention*, 425, 440–41, 464, 467–68.
61. Harris, *Pearl S. Buck*, 88–89.
62. Ibid., 91–93.

63. Ibid., 93–94.
64. Ibid., 94–96; a copy of her rough and final drafts of this letter can be found in Pearl S. Buck to the Editor, *Manchester Guardian*, January 22, 1948, CJH, Box 2, Folder 8, pp. 1–3.
65. Pearl S. Buck to Dr. Raphael Lemkin, February 3, 1948, CJH, Box 1, Folder 1, pp. 1–2.
66. Pearl S. Buck to Dr. Raphael Lemkin, February 11, 1948, CJH, Box 1, Folder 1; Pearl S. Buck to Dr. Raphael Lemkin, February 28, 1948, CJH Box 1, Folder 1, pp. 1–2; Gabriela Mistral to Pearl Buck, March 11, 1948, CJH, Box 1, Folder 1; Pearl S. Buck (Mrs. Richard J. Walsh) to Dr. Raphael Lemkin, March 20, 1948, CJH, Box 1, Folder 19, pp. 1–2; Pearl S. Buck (Mrs. Richard J. Walsh) to Dr. Raphael Lemkin, April 16, 1948, CJH, Box 1, Folder 19, pp. 1–2.
67. *Genocide Convention*, 493.
68. Ibid., 979–1010.
69. Cooper, *Raphael Lemkin*, 126–28, 130–37.
70. Harris, *Pearl S. Buck*, 97.
71. *Genocide Convention*, 1219–51.
72. Harris, *Pearl S. Buck*, 97–98.
73. *Genocide Convention*, 1284, 1354–1501.
74. Lemkin, *Totally Unofficial*, 172–73.
75. *Genocide Convention*, 1775, 1864–1942, 2022–91.
76. Lemkin, *Totally Unofficial*, 177.
77. Steven V. Roberts, "Reagan Signs Bill Ratifying U.N. Genocide Pact," *New York Times*, Nov. 5, 1988, 1.
78. Harris, *Pearl S. Buck*, 98–99; William Korey, *An Epitaph for Raphael Lemkin* (New York: Jacob Blaustein Institute for the Advancement of Human Rights, 2001), 61.
79. Harris, *Pearl S. Buck*, 99.

CHAPTER 2

Pearl Buck and the Evolution of American Foreign Policy: Reflections and Speculations of Her Film Biographer

Donn Rogosin

It is fairly easy to imagine the elation Pearl S. Buck would have felt at the election of President Barack Obama. It would have pleased her that a man of brown skin had finally achieved the highest political office in the land. During the 1930s and 1940s she had been an important voice in the increasingly vocal civil rights movement. As perhaps the most visible white member of the NAACP she had written for the organization's magazine *Opportunity*, and Walter White, then head of the NAACP, had referred to her as one of the few prominent whites who really "understood" the plight of the black man in America. As she herself said, "I've a very close feeling for [the Negros'] situation because I remember what it was like to be considered inferior," referring to her own upbringing as a girl in China where her white skin and blue eyes were not the privileged colors.[1]

She would undoubtedly have smiled when reflecting on the future president's childhood: the offspring of a complicated multiracial union; raised in racially diverse Hawaii, with significant overseas time as a youngster in Indonesia, a majority Muslim country of Asia; yet in many ways molded by his mother and grandparents' Kansan roots.

However, as a filmmaker who had the joy of documenting her remarkable life and recording many interviews with individuals who had known her well plus scholars who had studied her life and writing, I began to speculate on what Pearl Buck would think about American foreign policy during the Obama presidency. What kind of role had her extraordinary prolific career as a public intellectual and spokesperson for Asia played in the evolution of American foreign policy?

My cerebral journey was touched off by a comment that Jim Thomson made on camera during our production of *East Wind, West Wind: Pearl Buck, the Woman Who Embraced the World.* Jim's mother, Margaret Thomson, was Pearl Buck's best friend in Nanking (now Nanjing), and Jim called Pearl Buck "Auntie Pearl." His career included posts as a member of the National Security Council, head of the Neiman Fellows at Harvard University, and advisor to presidents. While working for Undersecretary of State Chester Bowles, he said, "Pearl came to Washington to warn the State Department that a coup in Korea was imminent and that Korean democracy was at risk."

Few Americans knew Korea the way Buck did, and she was correct, for shortly thereafter a military coup toppled the government in a bloody episode that reverberates to this day. "To Pearl's great credit she wanted to use her influence for what we call today 'human rights,'" Thomson said.

Human rights, as projected during Obama's terms, was an ideal at the heart of Pearl Buck's worldview but also central to Obama's foreign policy. By that I mean emphasis on individual rights as separate from the rights of sovereign states; equality for women and special status for children; protections for the disabled, the disadvantaged, and refugees; a belief in international law and diplomacy exercised within international organizations; an emphasis on people-to-people exchange and nongovernmental organizations that promote transparency and democracy; the projection of soft power; and the building up of what today would be called civil society. When did all these ideas, lumped together nowadays under the umbrella of "human rights," become essential elements of American foreign policy, and could Pearl Buck have had a role in its flowering, I wondered?

Laying the Foundation

American foreign policy had an immaculate conception in George Washington's farewell speech to the nation. "Europe has a set of primary interests which to us have none or very remote relations," Washington declared. It was "unwise" to get involved in foreign entanglements, he cautioned.[2] But soon enough there were foreign issues aplenty to deal with, such as Barbary pirates, the Napoleonic Wars, the War of 1812, and the national debt. The isolationist impulse became deeply embedded in both policy and practice from the very beginnings of the nation. The Monroe Doctrine in 1823 might be the fitting capstone to this early period, essentially telling Europeans, "hands off our hemisphere." The corollary received equal standing: America wanted nothing to do with the convulsive machinations of the "Great Powers" during Europe's turbulent nineteenth century.

America's main direction in the nineteenth century was westward. This expansionist policy had enormous consequences for Mexico, who saw half their territory incorporated into the United States, and a few scares for Canada as well. But, it pretty much stopped at the water's edge—until, that is, near the end of the nineteenth century, when the United States swiftly put an end to imperial Spain, annexed the Hawaiian Islands, sided with seven other imperial powers in putting down the Boxer Rebellion in China, and demanded huge reparations from China.

The experience of the Boxer Rebellion seems to have had a large impact on young Pearl because, even at an early age, she understood that the upheaval building in Asia could not be contained. Her Chinese tutor had cautioned that she needed to make her life as an American because the Asians would not be distinguishing between good foreigners—meaning in Pearl's young eyes, Americans—and imperialistic ones like the British, German, Japanese, and other colonial powers that had taken advantage of Chinese weakness. Pearl was proud that her parents had immersed themselves in Chinese life, unlike those nearby neighbors living in the British and French enclaves situated on the hills above her town of Zhenjiang (then Chingkiang). "I was old enough to read history myself and to see that Chinese historians and English historians gave entirely different versions of not only the same events but that each despised each other as a lesser breed," Pearl said.

Certainly that was the opinion of President Theodore Roosevelt, who had described the Chinese as an "immoral, degraded, and worthless race."[3] Roosevelt's views were completely at odds with the missionaries' views of the Chinese, which Harvard's John Fairbank characterized as a "deserving people who could be saved for Christianity, but had a long way to go."

Pearl Buck combined in her upbringing the intellectualism of her brilliant, harsh father, Absalom Sydenstricker, who had made the first Chinese translation of the Bible, with the gentle, inclusive Christianity of her mother, who had been raised as a Mennonite. The location of their mission was fortuitous as well since Zhenjiang was a significant trading port at the intersection of the mighty Yangtze River and the Grand Canal, and the site of important historic conflicts between the Chinese and European powers. The squabbles, rivalries, and animosities among the foreign powers often were mimicked by the Westerners posted to China, whether missionary, businessperson, or minor government official. This remote but strangely cosmopolitan outpost of late-nineteenth-century Western civilization sensitized Pearl to the petty, often ignorant attitudes that incubated and also emotionalized the power struggles of nations.

Time and time again Buck's humanistic appreciation of foreign peoples, rooted in her childhood years in China, surfaced in her concern that American policy was working against American interest. To her, with the Christian mindset of her upbringing, this was primarily due to a misunderstanding or lack of knowledge about other cultures, and not just different national interests. The theme of cultural misunderstanding appears often in her writing and speeches. That assessment, spawned in the immediate aftermath of the Boxer Rebellion and reinforced by her own experience at Randolph-Macon Woman's College in Virginia (where her schoolmates seemed totally uninterested in her Chinese background), motivated her zeal to educate both Americans and non-Americans about each other's culture. Indeed, even the missionary lifestyle of her parents, moving back and forth between China and America, sometimes by way of Russia and northern Europe, internationalized her from her earliest days. The multinational mixture of foreigners in China gave her a worldly outlook within the trappings of a simple missionary lifestyle.

However, there was a certain irony in her positions because of the strong Southern Presbyterian missionary culture in which she grew up. After all, her home church was a branch of the Presbyterian Church that had split over the issue of slavery and come down on the side of the Confederacy.

But then, that irony would be magnified much more in the son of a Southern Presbyterian minister who assumed the presidency in 1912. Woodrow Wilson was the single most important figure in helping establish the groundwork for the human rights agenda, but was primarily known for his most significant failures: the lost peace of World War I and the lost fight for America's place within the League of Nations.

Isolation Meets Reality

Wilson's route to an internationalist approach was foreshadowed in a 1906 speech in which he said, "Soon the shores of Asia and then autocratic Europe shall hear us knocking at their back door, demanding admittance for American ideas, customs, arts."[4] In these words we hear the same morally superior tone that epitomized the emerging American approach to foreign nations, whether under Wilson or Presidents Theodore Roosevelt or William Howard Taft, a strand that found its most explicit presentation in Henry Luce's championing of the "American Century," and perhaps lingers still in the rhetoric about American exceptionalism.

America supported the "Open Door" policy in China, not desiring territorial concessions but demanding access for our businessmen. Rather than joining the Great Power alliances, the American stance was to use foreign policy to advance American business interests in the belief that dollar diplomacy was the most effective diplomacy. A telling illustration of the convoluted impulses in American policy was in America's decision to use the exorbitant reparation payments from the Boxer Rebellion indemnity for scholarships for Chinese students to come to America and study.

The traditional fear of foreign entanglements was so strong that despite Wilson's personal support for England during the early years of World War I, Wilson remained true to the isolationist-dominated mood of the American public. It took a series of shocks—including the sinking of American merchant ships, the famous Zimmerman telegram, and the realization that the fate of his deeply admired parliamentary democracy might hinge upon the United States entering the war—that somewhat reluctantly forced Wilson to commit American forces.

Wilson's struggle with the cunning victorious Allied powers of World War I is well documented, and his losing battle for a more generous peace has frequently (indeed, usually) been cited as sowing the seeds of the Second World War.[5] However, Wilson's Fourteen Points, his legalistic explanation of America's war aims, doesn't come close to the basic human rights agenda of the Obama presidency. The Fourteen Points was mostly concerned with the adjustments of diplomatic processes and territorial issues to the benefit of the victors, with its final point the establishment of a League of Nations.

For Buck, this formative epoch of American foreign policy was material to analyze and reflect upon. She had a helper in this regard in her brother Edgar. He had served with the League of Nations as an epidemiologist doing truly groundbreaking, historic work on public health issues. Pearl Buck cites her brother as educating her about the great tragedy of the American departure from the League of Nations, calling it "at worst a disaster and at best a postponement of . . . common sense."[6] Although Edgar died in the 1930s, it was not before playing an important role in the establishment of Social Security legislation and helping his increasingly prominent sister realize the critical importance of international institutions for the future world order.

Of course, Buck's views did not emerge in a vacuum. The very influential Carnegie Endowment for World Peace was created in 1910, and its leadership was instrumental in guiding Wilson's thinking and that of others throughout the years between World War I and World War II. Clearly, the liberal thought of the time was a significant influence on Buck as she avidly absorbed the main currents of the new internationalism swirling again the tide of conservative, isolationist America during her Nanjing years.

The core goal of internationalist thought from the initial Japanese attack on Manchuria in 1931 through the early 1940s, was to build a collective capacity in an international organization, an organization robust enough to deter war. In short, an organization with real power and not just a debating society. But it did not include an emphasis on human rights within its mission. Rather, it sought to rectify the perceived failures of the League of Nations, which had proved miserably inept in deterring Japanese, German, and Italian aggressive actions in the 1930s. Indeed, it was only when the immense horror of the Second World War, with its genocide, its massive refugee creation, its enormous toll of predominantly civilian dead and injured became manifest that the human rights agenda took hold.

The Return to America

When Buck returned to the United States in the 1930s, her agenda focused on genuine human rights: racial and gender equality, anti-colonialism, and above everything else, supporting the Chinese people as they battled with Japan. Her particular interest was aiding refugees, not trying to fortify military positions or serving as an apologist for the Chinese government.

Throughout the 1930's, with China in the daily newsreels due to the ferocious conflict with Japan and the hapless Western response, and in significant measure because of Buck's tireless efforts, American sympathy for China and the Chinese grew. According to Peter Conn, Pearl was extremely active in "almost all of America's non-governmental dealings with China." And, of course, with the Japanese attack on Pearl Harbor, her views on China became even more sought after by opinion leaders.

The powerful America affinity for China was not only of Pearl's making. It was built on a long-standing American interest in China that had its origins in the increasingly important business ties during the nineteenth century and the missionary movement that flourished with increasing intensity in the second half of the nineteenth century and the first half of the twentieth. Today American youngsters aren't told to eat their vegetables and clean their plates because "children are starving in China," but that expression became a cliché precisely because it was so often invoked throughout the twentieth century. (As a personal note, my mother fed me that line many times, along with a steady diet of Pearl Buck books in response to my request for something to read.) Raising money for Christian missionary work in China was a common Sunday church appeal.

However, it was Pearl Buck's works—first the moderately successful novel *East Wind: West Wind*, followed by *The Good Earth*, then the movie version of the latter which won a Best Actress Academy Award for Luise Rainer in 1937, and finally the enormous publicity that resulted when Buck was chosen as the first American woman to win the Nobel Prize for Literature in 1938—that gave energy and passion to that affection. In Jim Thomson's elegant expression, "She put a face on faceless China."

Pearl Buck's commitment and devotion to the home of her youth never wavered. At first she helped to organize United China Relief, providing aid for the millions of Chinese refugees displaced by the Japanese/Chinese war, and building teaching hospitals behind the Chinese front lines. Later during World War II, Buck spearheaded the move to use the war as a rationale to repeal the racially motivated Chinese Exclusion Act of 1922.

University of Michigan historian Harriet Mills, a daughter of Nanking missionaries, observes that Buck ran the campaign, financed the campaign, and celebrated the repeal of the Chinese Exclusion Act almost single-handedly from her office at the John Day Company headquarters on Broadway in New York City. Along with her husband, John Walsh, Buck took over and supported the influential *Asia* magazine, a monthly that, under their visionary leadership, sought to inform Americans about Asian developments and introduced Americans to such important future political and cultural leaders as Jawaharlal Nehru and Lin Yutang.

Perhaps a more telling example of both her influence and relevance depended on the very strong bond between Buck and First Lady Eleanor Roosevelt. Though they had met briefly in the 1920s, only after Buck returned to the United States in the 1930s did she begin a vital political friendship with Mrs. Roosevelt around their shared views on policy matters on race, gender, children, refugees, and developments in China and Asia. Most important, we know Mrs. Roosevelt communicated Buck's insights directly to the president. One illustration of this occurred in the lead-up to the creation of the United Nations where Mrs. Roosevelt played such a significant role in charting a course for the fledgling organization. It involved nothing less than the role China would play in the future United Nations.

In the discussions about the makeup of the future U.N. Security Council, the United States wanted China to be included as a permanent member, but this was not the desire of the Churchill-led British wartime government, which already was thinking of Britain's place in the postwar world. Would the British Empire, where the sun never set, be put back together, or would India, the African colonies, Malaysia, go their separate ways? Buck had been outspoken throughout the war years in pushing the view that the American war aims should be democracy, freedom, and especially independence for the former colonies of Britain and France, and these goals were most decidedly not the views of Winston Churchill or Charles de Gaulle's French "government in exile," for that matter. She refused to allow a war that she wholeheartedly supported to detract from her insistence that her racial and gender agenda not be delayed. In Peter Conn's summation, "Pearl Buck seemed to be one of the few Americans who understood the elementary connection between the nation's domestic behaviors and its foreign policy."[7]

The issue came to a head in 1943, when it became clear the Allies would eventually prevail and preparations for the post–World War II era commenced in earnest. At that time, the British wanted a Security Council without China. However, British Foreign Minister Anthony Eden reported that Roosevelt would be "suspicious" of any organization made up of only European and American countries, and that he (Eden) had "the strong impression that it is through the feeling for China that the President is seeking to lead his people to the concept of international responsibilities."[8]

Feeling for China? Who but Buck was most responsible for that feeling? She had burst upon the literary scene with *The Good Earth* at a time when the entire world was hungering for information about China. As John Fairbank observed, "it was at that point that she met up with history." Simply put, the international community wanted to know much more about China, and it was through Pearl Buck's eyes that they learned about the Middle Kingdom. For many decades after the publication of *The Good Earth*, Pearl Buck remained America's most translated author after Mark Twain, a strong indication of her global impact.

While the wartime Allies were debating and creating the future institutions of the postwar architecture, Buck was playing an informal role as advisor to her friend Eleanor Roosevelt, and by association President Roosevelt, on Chinese matters. Buck apparently had a good deal to do with raising President Roosevelt's doubts about the long-term viability of the Chiang Kai-shek government. Buck felt instinctively that the Communists would win the war for the hearts and minds of the pragmatic Chinese peasantry. She was able to communicate with the president directly through personal letters about China that were requested by her good friend Eleanor Roosevelt.

When Madame Chiang Kai-shek toured America in 1943, she received an overwhelmingly positive reception from her audiences: thirty thousand at the Hollywood Bowl and a joint session of Congress to which she gave an invited address, but not, interestingly enough, from President Roosevelt, who "couldn't wait to get her out of the country." His opinion was clearly reinforced by the twelve-page memo Buck sent Mrs. Roosevelt as a briefing on the Chinese situation, which included the recommendation that Chou En-lai's views be solicited to better understand the real situation on the ground in wartime China.

Her Hymnal Was Human Rights

Pearl Buck used the wartime years to expand on her belief in what later came to called "soft power." Perhaps the finest expression of this vision was her creation of the East-West Association, an educational and cultural effort that brought together Asians and

Americans and was intended to promote understanding between East and West. Its activities included distributing reading lists to schools and sponsoring conferences and lectures. In short, it wasn't overtly political. As Erik Barnouw, a participant in these activities, remarked, "she felt that the peace in the world in the future would depend on the extent the East and West could understand each other." Buck simply said, "We are one world, and if we don't know it, it's dangerous."

In the euphoria resulting from the Allied victory in World War II her ideas were popular. But they quickly became less so once the Cold War took hold. And much of the recrimination of that period came down to the argument about how and why China was "lost."

If President Roosevelt was not seduced by Madame Chiang Kai-shek's fabled beauty and charm, he was very much aware of the American people's interest in the fate of China. So too was his successor, President Harry Truman, who had to cope with the fallout from the Chinese Communist victory in 1949. As historian David McCullough noted, it was against the backdrop of a country that had developed its image of China in part from Buck's popular writings that Truman tried to explain the loss of China.[9] Truman commissioned a famous study of the events leading up the Communist victory, which squarely placed the blame on the nationalists' corruption and incompetence and not the lack of arms or men. Poor Truman was confronted with a binary choice: accept the Communist victory or engage in a land war in Asia, a choice that also split his generals.

The argument about who lost China was framed by the views of two children of China missionaries—Pearl Buck and Henry Luce. Luce, who had become America's most important newspaper magnate, was as devoted to China as Buck, and he used his newspapers to push opinions that were diametrically opposed to Pearl's. For Luce, the nationalist defeat was primarily due to the sowing of doubt about Chiang Kai-shek from China experts such as Buck and those she knew well in the State Department and within universities and even the military.

James Michener observed that Luce, "with all his great power . . . had sided with Chiang Kai-shek . . . and he felt that anybody with any sense who didn't follow him was a traitor or perhaps a communist." His diagnosis was that some Americans had been deceived by the Communists and had weakened the anti-Communist forces. This had repercussions throughout the Cold War–dominated milieu of the 1950s, a time in America when Buck was among America's most prominent liberals.

Journalist Ross Terrill, who wrote the definitive book about Madame Mao, assessed it this way: "Pearl Buck was really a Confucian. . . . She did not think that Maoism amounted to what it claimed. In that sense, she was fundamentally against the Chinese communists," but she knew Chiang Kai-shek far too well to defend him. Jim Thomson said, "It was to her great credit that she did not feel that our culture, and our politics, and our system had the answer for everyone else. Henry Luce never doubted it!"

Along with other outspoken liberals of the 1950s, such as Eleanor Roosevelt and Buck's friend Congresswoman Helen Gahagan Douglas, Buck went from the insider of the 1940s to a fringe public intellectual of the 1950s. In fact, she became a target for the FBI in the witch-hunting hysteria of the 1950s where her FBI dossier was two hundred pages long. Always quotable and readily available, her opinion that "the great thing Russia has created is an alternative to empire" didn't help her during the dark days of the Cold War.[10]

Pushed from the limelight and national arena, she was never one to stand still. She bravely became a staunch supporter of the American Civil Liberties Union during the Joseph McCarthy era, and spoke and wrote forcefully of the dangers of nuclear war and the importance of disarmament. She advocated dialogue with and understanding about the Soviet Union at a time when such views went against the mainstream attitudes. And she argued forcefully that the emerging forces of Asia would come down on the Soviet side if the United States didn't reject the recolonization efforts of Britain and France and put an end to racial discrimination in the

United States, views that were prescient, but extremely unpopular at the time.

In a sense Pearl Buck was a Christian soldier whose hymnal was human rights. Harriet Mills explained that "she wanted to advance the human causes for good. She'd probably hate that word. The human causes she felt could bring about peace and harmony and justice in the world. . . . in one way or another, whatever you call it, it's the same missionary impulse." And James Michener observed that "the fact that she won this great prize, and that her books were so widely disseminated, gave her a special position and (that) she would be delinquent if she didn't utilize it."

But Buck was also a determined pragmatist. If the national stage restricted her influence from the 1950s and beyond, she would find worthwhile outlets for her seemingly boundless energies. Nothing illustrates this aspect of her character more than the development of Welcome House, an organization that took in unwanted children, often the result of mixed race relationships between American servicemen and Asian women. Later, this effort morphed into the Pearl S. Buck Foundation, an international adoption agency initially focused on Asia.

Women, First and Always

Of course, the reason Buck had a stage at all was because of her writing and her unique position as the first American woman to win the highest award in world literature, the Nobel Prize. Essentially every topic of importance to her received a literary treatment: *The Good Earth* (China), *The Living Reed* (Korea), *Mandala* (India), *Command the Morning* (nuclear disarmament), and *The Child Who Never Grew* (the mentally handicapped). And, invariably, the subject was also the role of women in a changing society.

Buck was clearly born to be a writer. Every observer of her life, whether close and personal or scholarly and professional, discusses her childhood interest in books and in writing, beginning with submissions to the missionary board publications as a child. She won prizes and recognition for her writing from her earliest days through college and went on to write occasional articles while still the missionary wife of her first husband, noted agricultural scientist John Lossing Buck. Buck's first writing of major note was an essay in 1924 for the *Nation* called "In China Too." But, as Peter Conn pointed out, even in this very first work her central focus was the status of women in a culture undergoing profound cultural change.[11]

And as her friend Michener commented, "one of the crucial experiences of her life was being in China and seeing the low status of women, just as cattle almost. She saw a great deal of that and wanted no part of it." Today, the gender issue is a major focus of American foreign policy initiatives, particularly through the Agency for International Development (AID), and also through persistent efforts of a plethora of activities public and private around the world. But in Buck's time there was none of this.

Buck was highly polemical in her argument for women rights, taking views that were not just controversial, but almost taboo in the 1930s, such as support for her friend Margaret Sanger's efforts in birth control. Indeed, throughout Buck's public life she was perhaps the most popular culture advocate for rights for women. In the 1930s, 1940s, and 1950s she insistently made the case, in the words of her collaborator Ted Danielewski, "that women's potential was not being used." During those decades, she was not only the most popular woman writer but also her books had a very special appeal to women readers. Part of that attraction was that she wrote about issues that spoke to women—matters that were not being covered in the elite male world of writers at the time. Why was Pearl so popular with women especially? As Jane Rabb of Radcliffe College observed, "She was a real role model. Here was a successful author, happily married wife, mother of many children, and there was a lot of tragedy which she dealt with and publicized. People could identify."

When I would present my film *East Wind, West Wind* to audiences and include a question-and-answer session, I would notice that the audiences were always well represented by women of an older generation. Tipped off by Jane Rabb, I'd ask if they remembered any particular scenes that spoke to them in Buck's books. Invariably I would hear about the scene in *The Good Earth* where the heroine working in the fields lies down, gives birth to a baby, and returns to work!

Adjusting to a New Era

If the 1950s were not particularly kind to Pearl Buck, she, like so many other liberals of her time, greeted the Kennedy administration with some optimism. She had a strong dislike for Richard Nixon, who had risen to prominence in part because of his ferocious attack on her friend Congresswoman Helen Gahagan Douglas. And some of the earliest actions of President Kennedy did not disappoint. In particular, the establishment of Agency for International Development in the earliest days of the Kennedy presidency signaled his willingness to engage in the battle for hearts and minds, something Buck had been doing her entire public life. The premise that foreign aid was an essential tool of foreign policy was a real departure from the predominant dollar diplomacy of the past, and while it built upon FDR's "Good Neighbor" policy for Latin America, AID envisioned a much more assertive intervention. Pearl's own emphasis on people-to-people engagement was reflected in Kennedy's extension of the Appalachian Volunteers program to the world through the Peace Corps. I would go a step farther and note that her East-West Association was a forerunner of President Obama's "People to People" diplomacy.

One might think the mischaracterized Camelot presidency would be the jumping-off point for the expansion of the human rights agenda, and in a sense it was, because unlike in previous administrations Kennedy enthusiastically endorsed the idea of a war for the hearts and minds of the world against the Soviet-led side in the Cold War.

One cannot possibly quantify or even measure Buck's contribution to the evolution of American foreign policy. What one can say definitively is that she was far ahead of her time in her views: that American foreign policy came around to her worldview and her agenda rather than vice-versa. One could go a step further in attribution. Her model of activism—finding a cause she believed in, and then organizing and mobilizing the public to do something about it—was trendsetting and a vital contribution to changing American policy itself. Wherever one looked during her American years, from 1931 to her death in 1973, she was influencing the future. And the issues on which she chose to devote her energies, such as mixed-race adoption, gender equality, and the norms of democracy and transparency, were ones that have now become mainstream.

Her Place in American Culture

So why has Pearl Buck dropped off the American cultural landscape in the twenty-first century? Partially it is because her literary output did not survive the direction of literature departments in the 1960s and swept through universities on both sides of the Atlantic. "There wasn't much there for the critics and academics to explain to anybody," said Rabb, who also noted the jealousy and sexism of many of Buck's literary naysayers. And even her biographers acknowledge that because she was fundamentally writing to finance her many causes, the literary output was uneven at best and some of her books, plays, and other literary endeavors really weren't very good. Even so, her cultural standing shouldn't depend on the value put upon her work by literature departments, though today more than ever literature departments are studying and evaluating the popular authors and their times.

In addition, with the rise of American studies departments and departments of popular culture, one would think that her opus would get a fresh look. Buck's inclusion in the curriculum belongs not only in literature departments, where she represents an important milestone in the history of American writing, but also in history, biography, popular culture, and above all American studies, which uses all the disciplines to illuminate the workings of American culture. By almost any measure her impact was huge. She was the most popular woman writer in the world for more than a decade, and probably the best paid as well.

And, though she wasn't a politician in any conventional sense, her life and work had enormous impact. When she won the Nobel Prize in Literature in 1938 at the age of forty-eight, the Nobel committee made a point of saying that the award was not exclusively for her signature novel, *The Good Earth*. They explicitly cited the biographies of her parents, *The Fighting Angel* and *The Exile*. These two books belong on any list of the greatest works of American literature, as well as being indispensable and informative documents of their time. Yet all acknowledge that the award fundamentally was for her role in humanizing China at the time of the Japanese attack upon China. It was essentially this internationally important cultural entity—the Nobel committee saying, in effect, "pay attention to China. We reward this work in bringing China to center stage in the world."

How interesting that Barack Obama, at the age of forty-six, received the Nobel Peace Prize for a similar contribution to the world's culture. Clearly Obama had not "deserved" the prize for the body of his work in 2009. But he did deserve the recognition in acknowledgment of the changes that had occurred in America during the lifetime of Pearl Buck and in the years that followed.

NOTES

Special thanks to Janet Sykes and the librarians of the Wilson Center, Washington, DC.

1. Quotes from the documentary *East Wind, West Wind: Pearl Buck, The Woman Who Embraced the World*, produced by Craig Davidson and

Donn Rogosin, aired June 20, 1993, on PBS, http://pearlbuckthedoc.com. Unless otherwise indicated, all quotations by Buck and other persons come from *East Wind, West Wind* and are not noted hereafter.

2. "Washington's Farewell Address," September 19, 1796, *The George Washington Papers Digital Edition*, ed. Theodore J. Crackel, et al. (Charlottesville: University of Virginia Press, Rotunda, 2007–), 26, http://gwpapers.virginia.edu/documents_gw/farewell/fwa26.html.
3. Peter Conn, *Pearl S. Buck: A Cultural Biography* (New York: Cambridge University Press, 1996), 32.
4. "Speech of March 22, 1906," in *The Papers of Woodrow* Wilson, vol. 16, 1905–1907, ed. Arthur S. Link (Princeton: Princeton University Press, 1974), 341.
5. See, for example, Richard Striner, *Woodrow Wilson and World War I: A Burden Too Great to Bear* (Lanham, MD: Rowman & Littlefield, 2014), 184, 215–220; and John A. Thompson, *Woodrow Wilson* (London: Taylor and Francis, 2002), 231.
6. Pearl S. Buck, *My Several Worlds: Abridged for Younger Readers*, ed. by Cornelia Spencer (New York: Day, 1957), 111.
7. Conn, *Pearl*, 290.
8. Anthony Eden, *The Reckoning* (Boston: Houghton Mifflin, 1965), 437.
9. David McCullough, *Truman* (New York: Simon and Schuster, 1993), 744.
10. Conn, *Pearl*, 291.
11. Conn, *Pearl*, 75.

CHAPTER 3

Pearl Buck's Strategic Vision: Decolonization, Desegregation, and Second World War Imperatives

Charles Kupfer

The future of colonies posed two sides of a nettlesome problem for percipient Americans thinking strategically during the Pacific phase of the Second World War. So troublesome was the matter that, to a large extent, even those who saw the issue as intrinsic to the fight as well as to any acceptable postwar arrangement in Asia tended to put it off in favor of Allied solidarity. That approach jibed with Winston Churchill's when he famously informed the House of Commons in 1942 that he had not become the king's first minister "in order to preside over the liquidation of the British empire."

India was foremost on his mind in that speech, but so too were Burma, Malaysia, and Singapore. During early 1942, each of the latter three fell under Japanese control, as did the Dutch East Indies. In Indochina, feeble Vichy French administrators retained some nominal authority, but only on Japanese sufferance. It was not clear whether even India would avoid falling under the implacably advancing Rising Sun banner. Meanwhile, Japan's army continued its inroads into China, and the navy ruled the western Pacific and eastern Indian Ocean. Opposing Japanese imperialism was of course an obvious Allied mandate that Americans supported. What was less clear was the future of Europe's Asian colonies, most of which had active independence movements, many weighing whether supporting Japan or the Allies represented a better path to independence. At this moment of maximum military peril for the anti-Axis nations, several renowned strategists weighed the issue in American public discourse. Few spoke clearly from the profound—and, as it turned out, correct—viewpoint that failure to mesh Allied war aims with Asian aspirations for postwar independence would lead to disaster. Even fewer drew a connection to racial policies at home. One who did speak precisely and fearlessly on these points was Pearl S. Buck.

Buck spoke by invitation on February 10 to the American Booksellers Association National Conference, held at the swank Hotel Astor, located on Broadway between Forty-Fourth and Forty-Fifth Streets, by Times Square. This was ten years after her Pulitzer Prize for *The Good Earth*, four years after her Nobel Prize in Literature, and one year after the publication of *China Sky*. At the time of her talk, Buck's publisher, John Day, was publicizing the release of her newest novel, *Dragon Seed*, portraying the travails faced by peasants caught up in the 1937 Rape of Nanjing (Nanking). Because of its specific setting and timeframe, *Dragon Seed* is less sweeping than some of her earlier works, but critics approved. "The family with whom we live during the hours we are reading *Dragon Seed* . . . are in themselves much more interesting, familiar, and likable, even lovable, than the rough peasants of *The Good Earth*," enthused the reviewer in *Book of the Month Club News*.[1] Alexander Brede, a professor at Wayne State, was also positive in his write-up for the *Far Eastern Quarterly*, although he admitted that the follow-up was "not so gripping as *The Good Earth*." This was a natural shortfall, he thought, because while she had "lived intimately the life in *The Good Earth* and long meditated upon it . . . she has not herself experienced the terrible situations which the Chinese have suffered lately." But the reviewer nevertheless found *Dragon Seed* rife with "excellent characterizations," populated by a family who embody "the hope, the energy, the resourcefulness of the Chinese; resist the enemy and till the land."[2] It is fair to term *Dragon Seed* the first sustained treatment of the Nanjing massacre to which Americans were widely exposed.

At this time, Buck was probably the leading and most trusted American source on all things Chinese. Her only possible peer was Brigadier General Claire Lee Chennault, then busily supervising the incorporation of the Flying Tigers All Volunteer Force into the United States Army Air Force.[3] So it was no surprise that she was asked to speak to the Booksellers Association about China. But Buck, never without her own voice, made a point of telling her audience that instead she aimed to talk about Asia in general, and the world at large. "China," she began, "is no more to be talked about as a separate entity in this world in which none of us is any more an individual or whole in himself. China has become a part of the world, the same world of which we are a part."[4] In other words, Buck aimed to deliver not a familiar and sure to be well-received homily on Chinese virtue and Japanese villainy but a frankly prescriptive strategic analysis of Asia, including China's role therein—and the United States' role as well. She would do this at exactly the moment when Allied war fortunes were at their all-time lowest. Indeed, this was the time during World War II when the war's outcome looked most propitious for the Axis.

The Allies in the Pacific at that moment faced one blur of concurrent disasters. Since the attack on Pearl Harbor, the Japanese had seized Hong Kong and Wake Island. They sailed brazenly through the Indian Ocean and South China Sea. Having landed Formosa-based invasion troops on Luzon, they moved swiftly through the Philippines. The US Navy's Asiatic fleet fled to temporary haven in Dutch Java, while General Douglas MacArthur maneuvered his forces away from Manila to defensive positions along the Bataan Peninsula. The Filipino capital fell on January 2, 1942. By the time Buck spoke in New York, American soldiers and marines were conducting a fighting retreat down Bataan, with the increasing realization that neither relief nor evacuation was forthcoming. These haggard troops fought bravely for time as they headed to Corregidor and eventual surrender in May. In the Dutch Indies, where the Allies hastily assembled the ABDACOM (American-British-Dutch-Australian Command), the situation was quite grim. Thirty thousand Dutch and a hundred thousand colonial Indonesian defenders resisted desperately but could not stem the Japanese advance toward Borneo's oil fields.[5] Later in February, a combined Allied fleet was annihilated by the Imperial Japanese Navy at the Battle of Java Sea. This was a humiliating defeat for the Americans. For the Dutch, the battle marked the effective end of control over their most prized colonies.[6]

The British had shifted their naval units to Malaya in a last-ditch attempt to salvage their defense of that peninsular colony and, at its tip, Singapore.[7] They were also coping, barely, with the invasion of Burma. Regarding Burma, one week before Buck's speech, American General Joseph Stillwell was typically acerbic. "The British have one brigade east of Rangoon and one more on the way. That's what they thought sufficient to hold Burma," the Anglophobic "Vinegar Joe" said with scorn: "The Supreme Commander, Wavell, refused Chiang K'ai-Shek's offer of two corps. Didn't want the dirty Chinese in Burma."[8] At the time of Buck's address, Japanese troops were well on their way to the mouth of the Irrawaddy River and preparing to capture Rangoon. Even worse for the British and Allied position, General Tomoyuki Yamashita's men coursed down Malaya despite British and Australian attempts to hold various defensive lines. Singapore, the "Gibraltar of the East," fell to the invaders on February 15 in the worst British defeat of the war.[9] That prompted Mollie Panter-Downes to blunt reflection in the *New Yorker*. "This is one of the bad moments in English history," she decided. "Although it had been regarded as inevitable, the fall of Singapore sounded to Britons something like an earth-shaking rehearsal for judgement day."[10] Reporter H. R. Knickerbocker, a Pulitzer Prize winner like

Buck, took in the whole cataclysm and foresaw the end of European rule in Asia. "No Asiatic loves the Japanese," he announced. "But their success would be bound to influence every Asiatic against the white man, and this would be true above all in India, which is a fact the British ought to be thinking about at this moment."[11]

Such was the backdrop Americans contemplated during that season of epic defeat. As Buck took the podium in the Astor's nicest ballroom, her audience was well aware that American involvement in the war was off to a deeply troubling start; Japanese power ran rampant across the Asian theater; even in the Atlantic, just off New York Harbor, German U-boats preyed upon defenseless and unprepared American ships. Victory in the war hardly seemed a foregone conclusion, and while national confidence remained high, it did take good perspective and no small amount of guts to presume to give a speech outlining Buck's vision. She had plenty of both.

Having informed her audience that she would not confine her remarks to China as originally expected, the author turned her attention to Japan. But in assessing the mindset that led Tokyo not just to depredations in China but also the attack against the United States, she identified two latent problems. The first was the propensity of Americans to care little about Asia and to pay it less-than-rapt attention. For too long, she suggested, Americans had labored under the mistaken calculus that British, French, and Dutch interests predominated there and could keep Japanese ambitions in check. Instead, she said, it was clear that the United States was the crucial Allied power, and the Pacific, rather than being a secondary war theater to Europe, was precisely where major American interests lay. "Even at this moment," she insisted, "Most Americans seem unable to grasp that actually the American stake in the Far East is far greater than it is in Europe. If the American way of life is to prevail in the world, it must prevail in Asia whether it prevails in Europe or not." Her point, which she developed at length, was that too many Americans were in thrall to "unreal and nostalgic" notions about European connections that, she insisted, were increasingly outmoded. "While the minds of Americans were preoccupied with English and European literature and tourist travel, our firmest political interests were not in Europe but in Asia."[12] The Japanese, she pointed out, were well aware of this. Their inroads to date could in part be explained by the lamentable fact that Tokyo saw American interests more clearly than Washington had, and was not hesitant to take advantage of this fact.

There was more than a kernel of truth at work here. Since the German invasion of Poland in September 1939, Americans had been fascinated with the Second World War. As the weeks of conflict stretched into months, American consumption of news from Europe was compulsive and sustained. Edward R. Murrow and the renowned crew of CBS radio correspondents in each European capital brought the sounds of war and latest developments into American living rooms. Newspapers covered the tactical and strategic dimensions of each battle and every move made by Adolf Hitler. Magazines speculated about future military developments. Whether isolationist and opposed to involvement, or interventionist and supportive of aiding Britain, more and more Americans came to believe that the war must involve them at some point. The economy was firmly in preparedness mode and factories tooled up to produce armaments under the Arsenal of Democracy rubric. The Third Reich was obviously malevolent and Hitler never enjoyed support among any statistically significant segment of the American populace, but he certainly was newsworthy. When the Nazis invaded Norway in April 1940, then Belgium, the Netherlands, and France on May 10, 1940, Americans watched in awe. France's fall that June provided one of the rudest shocks ever to popular assumptions about national security. Since 1918, Americans reckoned that the French Army and Royal Navy were, in essence, their first line of defense. With France out of the war and the British assailed from the air during the fall-winter 1940–41 Battle of Britain, it was no longer clear that Europe's dangers could be kept at bay. As the war wore on, it was events in Europe that transfixed the American public. This included the June 1941 Nazi invasion of the Soviet Union. So when the war actually struck from the east, in Hawaii, on December 7, 1941, it came as a massive surprise.

Buck's purpose in her speech was to remind Americans that they were attacked in the Pacific and that this was no accident, but rather an indicator of the region's importance. She and others that February already knew that the Allies considered Germany the major threat. The President had explained as much in several speeches. The White House hosted Churchill in December to coordinate military strategy. So Buck can be heard as giving a nudging reminder to leadership, public, and press that neglecting the Asian theater would be a dire mistake.

Among her points of caution was a note against being too closely identified with Britain. So successful had Churchill's visit been, so completely won over were politicians, public, and press corps by his bravura performance before a Joint Congressional Session and in numerous confabs with reporters, that Buck discerned a dangerous tide of Anglophilia. The problem was, she insisted, that London remained wedded to its outdated imperial control over subject colonies, including in an Asia that was ready for self-determination. The populace from China to the Philippines, from Java to Korea, was watching to see if the Americans were simply another opportunistic colonial power. "Today, the colored peoples are still waiting, still watchful," she observed.[13] Her use of the loaded term "colored peoples" can be understood to include Africans, and her message of anticolonialism certainly embraced that interpretation.

Here again, Buck feared that the Japanese were ahead. "The most dangerous human stupidity has been that of the white race in the baseless prejudice through which even the meanest of white creatures has felt he could despise a king if his skin were dark." Meanwhile, she pointed out, Japan was forging ahead with an "Asia for Asians" propaganda line. Despite claims in American media that the attacks on China or Malaya would necessarily alienate other Asians, Buck was not sanguine, because the Japanese had plenty of examples of Western racism to use. "Japanese propaganda cannot be lightly dismissed. It lies uneasily in the minds and memories of many at this moment who are still loyally allied with Britain and the United States, in the minds and memories of the colored peoples of Asia."[14]

These were percipient and courageous words, since she was foreshadowing a later theme, the links between racial justice at home and abroad. Racial ambiguities in either sector could sabotage the victory effort. African Americans were famously loyal during the war, enlisting and serving in great numbers. But domestic initiatives such as the Double V campaign ("Victory at Home, Victory Abroad") sought to pair a war against foreign racist powers with the mandate for racial fairness in the United States. This was a tough sell, but Buck recognized that merely pointing to the virulence of Nazi race policy was insufficient at home and around the world if the United States and its allies wished to embody and advance the cause of equality. In Asia, she pointed out, "Such minds realize that though Nazism may give them nothing but death, yet the United States and Britain have given them too little for life in the past and not even promises for the future. Not only peace aims are still unknown—war aims are unclear." Even pointing to Japanese racial conceptions would not fend off the Greater East Asia Co-Prosperity Sphere, she warned. The reason was that heretofore subject colonial peoples might well decide that Japan was an ally of temporary convenience, insofar as they helped toss out the European colonial powers. Once the British, French, and Dutch were gone, she supposed, Malayans, Vietnamese, and Indonesians might believe they could figure out how to handle the Japanese. In another passage representing her willingness to speak her truth even in the face of current trends, she warned against the whole-hog adulation that covered Churchill's visit and speeches. Walking side by side with the British in Asia, she warned, meant "to the colored peoples a formidable white imperialism more dangerous to them than anything even a victorious Japan can threaten."[15]

Given that the United States had minimal territorial aims in Asia, Japan's anti-Americanism was based upon frank appeals to racial consciousness among Asians. "Japan is trying to prove to them that freedom is the one thing they will not have if America wins. She is using the most vulnerable point in our American democracy, our racial prejudice, as her weapon." She summed up Tokyo's main message: "The colored peoples have no hope of justice and quality from the white peoples because of their unalterable racial prejudice against us."[16] Here was the pith of her warning. She forged an explicit connection between race prejudice and colonial assumptions of the whites' right to rule. For this reason, she argued, it would be morally wrong and strategically obtuse to shed American blood so as to restore the British and other European colonial systems.

Prior to the war, British efforts, American sympathies, and the general concern for the welfare of a partner democracy helped to build widespread support for aiding Britain as it stood alone against Hitler's *Luftwaffe* and an expected invasion. Buck gave no sign of objecting to that. What she warned against was blindly extending such pro-British sentiments to the new theater of war. There, the issue was colonialism and empire set against natural democratic aspirations. There, she explained, the United States needed to differentiate between supporting the local peoples and supporting renewed European rule. For this reason, Buck threw rhetorical cold water on some of the more lavish pro-London proposals, such as the Union Now movement backed by figures such as Clare Boothe Luce. Instead of creating a democratic union, she admonished, a too-close association with London would put Washington on the wrong side of "the gravest war we can yet imagine." First of all, it would make China feel abandoned. Continuing this thread, she wondered, "What can China, that oldest and most pragmatic of democracies, think of a white English-speaking union which excludes her at the very start? We may as well present Japan with battleships and bombers as to go on with a union which denies democracy at its very start."[17]

While the prospect of formal unification with Great Britain was never more than a wild proposal broached in the most heated moments of wartime, Buck's point was that adopting the cause of the British Empire would be a profound mistake. Here, she hammered at the most delicate point of contention between Franklin Delano Roosevelt and Churchill. The president grew very cautious about the prime minister's sensitivity to any suggestion that the war must end in decolonization, or that India's vast resources and labor force might be best mobilized if some promise of eventual independence was part of the package. Here, the divergent natures of American and British imperialism are illustrated. Prompted as much by parsimony as morality (running a colony was expensive and there was no congressional unity in favor of such outlays, especially during the Depression), the United States had already promised the Philippines eventual independence before the war came. Filipinos understood that they were fighting for more than a return to subject status. But Churchill was the redoubtable champion of British elements determined to cling to India and other imperial possessions.

Buck was careful not to verbally sabotage Britain's position *vis-à-vis* Germany. "It is only natural," she allowed, "that England should think most of Hitler, the wolf at her own door. It is to be expected that English minds cannot take seriously enough the full threat of Japan to us. Why should they, when Americans themselves have not taken Japan seriously enough, and do not take any Asiatic people seriously enough? Pearl Harbor and Manila are today awful witnesses of our ignorance."[18] Buck did not explicitly oppose the "Europe first" strategy. That might have been the last hope of isolationists intent on limiting American involvement in the conflict. But days after Pearl Harbor, Hitler took the decision away from Roosevelt by declaring war on the United States. Buck did not suggest that Americans ignore the Nazi Reich and its mad plans for conquest. What she argued for was a careful differentiation between American understanding of what Britain stood for in Europe, as opposed to what the British Empire stood for in Asia and Africa. In this vein, she was frank about the racial dimensions of the Second World War, and she fearlessly contextualized these for her audience at the Astor. The situation in Asia and at home was the same, she insisted, returning to her theme that the "colored peoples" were waiting, watching.

With that in mind, she said, the Japanese were watching, too. To her credit, Buck's racial awareness did not stop at American shores. "Yes, and it lies uneasy, too, in the minds and memories of many colored citizens of the United States who cannot deny the charge and must remain loyal in spite of it." Tokyo's bet was that racism was so endemic to the American mindset and political structure that Washington would never admit Asians to the company of independent nations. Democratic promises were only for whites. This was the dangerous message the United States needed to squelch, and the only way to do so was to provide clarity on the subject by avowing American commitment to democracy as a guiding principle for postwar Asia. "But can the United States provide such leadership," she asked, fatefully. "Japan is busily declaring that we cannot. She is declaring in the Philippines, in China, in India and Malaya that there is no basis for hope that colored peoples can expect any justice from the people who rule in the United States." Japan quite openly pointed to domestic antiblack segregation and violence to buttress their case, she said, and if that case was to be dismissed, it had to be on the basis of demolishing racism at home. "Every lynching, every race riot gives joy to Japan. The discriminations . . . against colored soldiers and sailors, the exclusion of colored labor in our defense industries and trade unions, all our social discriminations, are of the greatest aid today to our enemy in Asia. 'Look at the Americans,' Japan is saying to millions of listening ears, 'Will white Americans give you equality?'"[19]

With this bold challenge to her audience, and to American conceits about the unblemished national commitment to wage just war, Buck moved to her conclusions. Here, she nearly left Asia behind in her argument about imperative racial justice. "How can we integrate ourselves for democracy?," she demanded, citing racial segregation as "this division between our belief in democracy for all and our practice of democracy at home." She attributed this inconsistency not to hypocrisy but to oversight. "We Americans are not hypocritical except in small amusing ways," she argued. "Talk to any American and he honestly believes in equality and justice and giving everybody the rights of freedom. But mention to him the colored man and you will not believe your own ears. This cannot be the same man talking. 'No, the colored man cannot have the same treatment as the white man.' 'Why?' you inquire. 'Well, it just don't work that way.'"[20]

Embedded in her account are two facts: first, this absence of rationale was no longer sufficient to justify segregation; second, it gave succor to the enemy abroad at the very moment when Americans needed to mobilize all resources to defeat the Axis powers. To Buck, racial justice was not just a moral but also a strategic imperative. At a time when Americans were asked to subordinate many life concerns to the paramount goal of victory, she named racism as one of the institutions that needed to be junked. "If we are to persist blindly in our racial prejudices," she concluded, "We are on the wrong side in this war. We belong with Hitler. For the white man can no longer rule in this world unless he rules by totalitarian military force. Democracy, if it is to prevail at this solemn moment of human history, can only do so if it purges itself of that which denies democracy and dares to act as if it believes."[21]

Buck's message was undeniably uncompromising. It was also undeniably unfashionable at the time she gave it, for public discourse in the United States was awash with patriotic formulas designed to boost the war effort. Those addresses that did focus on matters such as the role imperialism would play in formulating strategy, or the nonconsonance between domestic racial segregation and a forthrightly ideological crusade against monstrous racial violence abroad, were so few as to make Buck's talk stand out all the more. It was featured in the next issue of *Vital Speeches of the Day*, a bimonthly that mostly ran reassuring military predictions ("Allies on Offensive Soon: The Broad Oceans Have Become Endless Battlefields," a radio fireside chat by President Roosevelt); calls for Anglo-American unity in the name of democracy ("We Shall Not Fail Now," a BBC talk by Churchill); appeals for citizen unity at home ("We Must Respond in a United Fashion," by Office of Civilian Defense executive James M. Landis); and more soothing takes on American values during war ("The Soul of Uncle Sam: We Are Seeing Ourselves," by Stanford professor Edgar Eugene Robinson).[22] Buck's was by far the most challenging and provocative speech in the magazine for a period of weeks, insofar as she did not modulate her anti-imperialism, anti-segregation call in the name of wartime message control.

Even other luminaries directly associated with the themes Buck tackled at the Astor had trouble matching her overall force and coherence. The strength of her talk lay in the fact that she aligned moral imperatives with military effort, arguing that the former would augment and empower, not dissipate and weaken, the latter. A counterpart was civil rights advocate W. E. B. DuBois. His voice on the American racial question was hugely important, and *Dusk of Dawn* had just been published in 1940. But DuBois's focus on white imperialism had led him to the unfortunate decision to back Japan's colonial aspirations, seeing them as the surest way to eject Europe from Asia. The problem with this, of course, was that it suggested that China should reconcile itself to Japanese domination. "I believe in Japan," DuBois had insisted. "It is not that I sympathize with China less, but I hate white European and American propaganda, theft and insult more."[23] That was, at best, a tone-deaf interpretation of Chinese pain in the face of Japanese atrocities; at worst, it betrayed a willingness to see China sacrificed in order to maintain his own ideological comfort. The proposition that China sacrifice itself in order to avoid giving succor to the West, and the concurrent assumption that Japanese imperialism was a positive development for Asians, was bizarre and offensive.[24]

DuBois's position removed him from reasonable consideration on the subject of China. But other civil rights leaders also found themselves caught between their goal of linking racial progress at home and the exigencies of wartime unity. When A. Philip Randolph, Bayard Rustin, and A. J. Muste attempted to organize a 1941 march on Washington to demand desegregation in wartime employment, contracting, and the armed forces, they were subjected to a full Roosevelt charm treatment. Invited to present their petition to the White House, they discussed their goals amicably with the president and left thinking they had the outline of a deal. They were thus rueful when Stephen Early, presidential press secretary, implied to reporters that the civil rights movement accepted that "the policy of the War Department is not to intermingle the colored and white enlisted personnel."[25] What Early did point to as progress was Executive Order 8802, the Fair Employment Act, signed into law by Roosevelt in June 1941, intended to end discrimination in defense hiring.[26]

On the other side of the color line, Buck's message against imperialism in Asia had an ally in the august personage of Walter Lippmann, the nation's foremost pundit and likely its top public intellectual. As Singapore fell, Lippmann surveyed the Pacific scene and determined that this was the tolling bell for Western colonialism in that part of the world. It was high time, he argued in his column, for "putting away the 'white man's burden.'" He wanted to see the Allies "purging themselves of the taint of an obsolete and obviously unworkable white man's imperialism." What Lippmann wanted to see was overt United States support for extending the recent United Nations declaration, aimed at restoring independence to Europe's conquered nations, to Asian nations as well.[27] So Lippmann's view of the need for Britain, France, and the Netherlands to divest themselves of the notion that Asia was "theirs," and to set their colonies free, was in line with Buck's. Unfortunately, his attitude toward domestic racial justice was compromised by the integral role he played in developing and supporting the legal framework within which the western American states were declared a war zone. Within a war zone, constitutional protections did not apply, which was the key point. The war zone measure provided the legal cover necessary for interning Japanese Americans. Lippmann's embrace of a legalism that meant that, technically, the constitutional rights of these innocents were not violated even as they were hauled off to camps, did him no credit.[28]

The point in comparing those who only saw part of the whole that Buck perceived so clearly is not simply to criticize their occluded moral and strategic vision. Rather, it is to credit the seamless integrity and strategic sense of Buck. As history would show, at this moment of supreme Allied danger, her prescription—which struck some as too much, too soon—was entirely correct. Indeed, to some extent, Washington knew it. While Roosevelt withdrew his tentative feelers to Churchill about loosening imperial claims on India, the United States displayed far less compunction after the war when pressuring the Dutch to abandon their military campaign to suppress Indonesian independence. So there was some official understanding that the United States could play a decolonizing role in a continent rife with independence movements.

To read Buck's speech today is to be tantalized by truths uttered memorably but at best partially heeded. Somewhere in American leadership during those parlous World War II times there was awareness that Western colonialism and domestic racial discrimination ill served the putative causes for which Americans fought. But that moral awareness was too often counterbalanced by a pragmatic willingness to trim justice in service to wartime compromises. Buck was right about the home front and Asia. At home, it would take until 1948 for the armed forces to desegregate, and until 1954 for the Supreme Court to decide *Brown v. Board of Education.* By coincidence, regarding Asia, 1954 was the year the United States made the fateful decision to pick up the gauntlet left at Dien Bien Phu by the French. The defeat of France by the Viet Minh pointed back to Buck's prediction that the age of colonialism in Asia was played out. But by 1954, Cold War complications, especially concerns about links between independence movements and Soviet-inspired Communism, caused American policy makers to turn away from the postcolonial verities raised by Buck. It had already frozen Americans out of revolutionary China. In Southeast Asia, the direction allowed local nationalists to claim that American involvement was an extension of the Western imperialistic impulse. This turned out badly for the United States and Indochina. But that later fact of history only underscores the moral and strategic precision that made Buck's February 1942 Astor Hotel analysis a creditable part of her overall writerly repertoire.

NOTES

1. Advertisement, *Harper's*, January 1942, 223.
2. Alexander Brede, review of *Dragon Seed by Pearl S. Buck, Far Eastern Quarterly* (Spring 1942): 390.
3. Charles Kupfer, *Indomitable Will: Turning Victory into Defeat from Pearl Harbor to Midway* (New York: Continuum, 2012), 162–64.
4. Pearl S. Buck, "The Asiatic Problem: The Colored People Are Still Waiting, Still Watchful," *Vital Speeches of the Day*, March 1, 1942, 303.
5. H. P. Wilmott, *Empires in the Balance: Japanese and Allied Pacific Strategies to April 1942* (Annapolis, MD: United States Naval Institute Press, 1989), 264–66.
6. Paul S. Dull, *A Battle History of the Imperial Japanese Navy, 1941–1945* (Annapolis, MD: United States Naval Institute Press, 1978), 68–88.
7. Henry H. Adams, *1942: The Year that Doomed the Axis* (New York: Paperback Library, 1967), 88–89.
8. Joseph Stilwell, *The Stilwell Papers* (New York: Da Capo, 1991), 31.
9. Kupfer, *Indomitable Will*, 197–204.
10. Mollie Panter-Downes, *London War Notes, 1939–1945* (New York: Farrar, Straus and Giroux, 1971), 204–7.
11. H. R. Knickerbocker, "Planes, Men, Send Them Quickly," *Chicago Sun*, February 24, 1942.
12. Buck, "Asiatic Problem," 303.
13. Ibid.
14. Ibid., 304.
15. Ibid.
16. Ibid.
17. Ibid.
18. Ibid.

19. Ibid., 304, 305.
20. Ibid., 305.
21. Ibid.
22. *Vital Speeches of the Day,* March 1, 1942, table of contents.
23. Gerald Horne, *Black and Red: W. E. B. DuBois and the African-American Response to the Cold War, 1944–1963* (Albany: SUNY Press, 1986), 10.
24. Kupfer, *Indomitable Will,* 252.
25. David Levering Lewis, *W. E. B. DuBois: The Fight for Equality and the American Century* (New York: Owl Books, 2001), 469.
26. Executive Order 8022, https://www.eeoc.gov/eeoc/history/35th/thelaw/eo-8802.html.
27. Akira Iriye, *Power and Culture: The Japanese-American War 1941–1945* (Cambridge, MA: Harvard University Press, 1981), 74–76.
28. Kupfer, *Indomitable Will,* 239–44.

Chapter 4

Chinese Culture "Going Global": Pearl S. Buck's Methodological Inspiration

Junwei Yao

Pearl S. Buck considered China to be her "fatherland." Although she was born in the United States, her "motherland," her parents brought her to live in China when she was a little baby. In the process of growing up, the Chinese language and culture became an indispensable part of her education; since she stayed in China for about forty years, she was very familiar with Chinese people in many walks of life. As a result, she wrote about them quite naturally when she took up her pen, with a focus on the Chinese peasants, that part of the Chinese people she knew best. Thanks to her great efforts in her literary creations and social activities, China, together with the country's people and culture, became far better known to the outside world with a much more objective and positive image.

However, Buck's writings, especially those pertaining to Chinese subjects, have not always been well accepted in China. In fact, a large percentage of the criticisms are most unfavorable, particularly those made in the 1950s and the 1960s when all of her works were banned in China. Not until the late 1980s were Buck and her writings reappraised in China with the advent of the national open-door policy. Since the 1990s, an increasing number of Chinese scholars and translators, including myself, have devoted themselves to studying and translating the major works of Pearl S. Buck. In fact, scholars have now translated into Chinese not only her representative novels—such as *The Good Earth* trilogy, *East Wind: West Wind*, *The Mother*, and *Dragon Seed*—but also her short stories and works of nonfiction, including her studies of Chinese novels. Besides translations, anthologies of Buck's literature have been compiled for courses designed for both undergraduates and postgraduates. I myself have started offering a graduate-level course entitled Pearl S. Buck Studies. The course has yielded positive results, and a couple of cohorts of students have received systematic training in the study of Buck. They are now researching Buck in a vigorous and fruitful way.

Meanwhile, there appears to be a renaissance of scholarship centered on Buck in China. From various critical perspectives, like new historicism, aestheticism, feminism, anthropology, comparative literature, and postcolonialism, Chinese scholars have given serious treatment to Buck and her writings, elevating her reputation in the process. As a result, Buck's intercultural writings have been reassessed more objectively, and her literary and cultural contributions are recognized more fully in China. In contrast to the past, she now occupies a high position in the Chinese encyclopedia on foreign literature, literary histories, histories of literary translation, monographs, and academic papers written by Chinese scholars. We also see Buck's rising fortunes reflected in academic conferences. Through the joint efforts of Chinese scholars, administrators from cultural institutions and local governments (Zhenjiang's municipal government in particular), and institutions outside of China (especially Pearl S. Buck International), about ten conferences have recently been held in the various cities in which Buck once lived. All of this academic activity has positively transformed Buck's reputation in China. No longer labeled as "an owl" or "a vanguard of the cultural invasion of American imperialism," as she was accused of being in the 1960s, she is regarded as a supportive friend of the Chinese people, a great novelist who treats Chinese subjects well, a scholar of the Chinese novel, a committed social activist, and a cultural "bridge" who devoted her entire life to intercultural understanding and ultimately the well-being of humankind.

At the beginning of the twenty-first century, the Chinese government spearheaded "Going Global," an initiative intended to spread Chinese literature, culture, and values around the world. The government in Beijing sees Going Global as vital to China's national interests, and multiple administrative bureaus have responded by enthusiastically developing programming. So far, many conferences and forums have been held and scholars and administrators have made great contributions to the theory and practice of Chinese culture and literature "going global." Chinese scholars, writers, and sinologists outside of China are invited to make joint efforts; meanwhile, *Chinese Literature Today,* edited by Howard Goldblatt, has been published and many Chinese journals and magazines have started to publish English editions. From those efforts, it is not difficult to see the enthusiasm on the part of the Chinese government, relevant institutions, and professionals. Going Global provides some of the context for Buck's resurgence in China.

It is constructive for Chinese culture and literature to go global. An international perspective will help the Chinese see their own culture—its strengths and weaknesses—more clearly. In a sense, the introduction of Chinese culture overseas will also be beneficial to the development and improvement of other cultures of the world. In fact, Chinese culture and literature have, to a certain extent, already entered the international arena, an entry best symbolized by Mo Yan's winning of the Nobel Prize in Literature in 2012. Although it is quite natural for Chinese culture and literature to go international, the export process presents challenges. It is not easy for any culture to reach an international audience effectively and to be understood and accepted by other nations' cultures and literatures. This is often true of Chinese culture and literature. Indeed, Chinese literature represents the life of the Chinese people and attempts to capture and convey their feelings and emotions. Thus, to translate

Chinese literature into foreign languages and cultures does not mean just the translation of the Chinese language itself but also the elements behind the language. This is a very complicated matter. As such, it is advisable to show respect to the principles of translation, to really understand the needs of other cultures and literatures and to learn from successful forerunners in the history of cross-cultural communication.[1] In this respect, we have a lot to learn from Buck. Her approach to cross-cultural communication is methodologically inspiring and worth invoking in the present context.

1. Introducing Chinese Culture in Her Fiction

The ancient Chinese said, "Grief and indignation will produce poets." The saying clearly illustrates the relations between an author's achievements and his or her mentality. So far as Pearl S. Buck is concerned, her cross-cultural writings arose, so to speak, from her indignation. Before she took up her pen, most Westerners were unfamiliar with China, the Chinese people, and Chinese culture. What was imprinted in their minds were some distorted images, such as Fu Manchu and Charlie Chan, together with some hearsay stories full of wild fantasy and exaggeration. In their imagination, China was a mysterious and evil country and Chinese people were irrational and impenetrable. In most Western novels and travel books about China they were described "as an archetype: men with long pigtails and women with bound feet, all skinny with running noses and dirty, ugly faces. Their deeds are always connected with theft, burglary, raping, plotting and assassinations. For centuries, this has been the image the Western mind has of the Chinese."[2] Out of indignation, Pearl S. Buck was determined to present the Chinese people and Chinese culture in a compassionate way to the West. She hoped to use her cross-cultural writings to get rid of the prejudices some Westerners had about Chinese culture and people, and to help them see that Chinese people were not unreasonable heathens, that they also had their own pleasure, anger, sorrow, and joy, and that they were also humans with a common humanity living in the cultural traditions that were formed and kept over centuries, equally valid and understandable, though different from the Western ones.

For Buck, the criterion with which to define a nation's identity is not its geographical location nor its race but its culture and collective consciousness. The daily lives of the Chinese people are intricately and inextricably linked with their own culture; to understand Chinese people one has to understand Chinese culture. Unfortunately, since all people are shaped by culture, it is difficult to break away from it. Buck was fully aware of that, and so in her fiction she not only created Chinese characters in her genuine way but also created them by placing them in their own cultural environments so that her novels like *The Good Earth* trilogy, *East Wind: West Wind*, *Pavilion of Women*, and *Kinfolk*, among other works, are laden with elements of Chinese culture. In other words, she created such unforgettable characters as Wang Lung and O-lan, but at the same time she introduced a large number of Chinese elements such as Chinese marriage, family, and the core values of Chinese culture. Wang Lung starts as a very poor peasant, but with the help of O-lan and through their hard work, he gradually becomes rich and prosperous. He later mercilessly deserts his wife, but when she is dead he becomes conscience-stricken, and he repents. "Although he is dominated by a ruling passion for the land, he is above all a human being with all the whims, emotions, quirks, inconsistencies, contradictions and variable attitudes that go to make a living individual."[3] What is noteworthy is that Wang Lung is placed in the Chinese cultural environment, and the novel shows that he is formed by Chinese customs and habits.

Pearl Buck possessed a deep knowledge of the Chinese family, which she conveyed through literature. She lived her early years in China and was tutored by Mr. Kung, a Chinese Confucian scholar. In *The Good Earth* trilogy, she portrayed the ups and downs of three generations of the Wangs so that Western readers clearly could see their attitudes toward life, love, and family; as a result, the trilogy turns out a grand family history. *East Wind: West Wind* dramatically shows the conflicts between the old and the new in a traditional family. *Pavilion of Women* tells a story about an extended family of property, where three generations plus servants live—more than sixty members in all. In *Kinfolk*, Buck describes for us another traditional family; though this time the entire family lives in the United States in the beginning, Chinese cultural elements are abundantly exhibited. Finally, *The First Wife and Other Stories* also represents Buck's effort to reveal Chinese cultural messages by describing the scenes of the lives of Chinese families.

Buck understands that Chinese families are the foundation of the Chinese society. That is why the very first sentence of *The Good Earth* is "It was Wang Lung's marriage day."[4] A new family is going to be set up. Wang Lung is getting ready to meet and take home his bride, O-lan. After some twists and turns, he succeeds in taking her from the House of Hwang. On their way home, the bridegroom burns some incense before the earthen gods. And in the evening, some villagers, friends, and relatives, including his paternal uncle and cousins, come to Wang Lung's wedding celebrations. However, it is the bride who prepares the dishes. Certainly, she does not appear before the guests since she is not supposed to be seen by strangers until after their wedding night.

In describing the Chinese familial system, Buck introduced to Western readers the custom of arranged marriage so prevalent in traditional China. In traditional Chinese society, an arranged marriage was taken for granted. Marriages were not merely individual matters but were closely related to the prosperity and continuity of a family clan. "The contract in a legal civil marriage in China is not between the woman and the man," writes cultural historian Ku Hung Ming. "The contract is between the woman and the family of her husband. She is not married to him, but into the family."[5] What's more, Chinese people used to get married at an early age, so parents' or intimate seniors' roles seemed all the more important in such a big matter as marriage. In fact, Chinese parents were exercising their responsibility out of a sense of duty at critical moments like this.

Wang Lung's marriage to O-lan is one example of an arranged marriage. Their marriage is arranged by his father and the Old Mistress of the House of Hwang. He is an impoverished farmer and therefore cannot afford to get married to a maiden from a respectable family. What remains for the poor like him are only slaves. When his father says that he is going to find a slave neither too young nor pretty, he becomes so disappointed as to contest his father's act. "It would have been something to have had a pretty wife that other men would congratulate him upon having." What Wang Lung has in his mind is entirely human, though somewhat vain. Being more practical, his father cries at him: "And what will we do with a pretty woman? We must have a woman who will tend the house and bear children as she works in the fields, and will a pretty woman do these things? She will be forever thinking about clothes to go with her face! No, not a pretty woman in our house. We are farmers."[6] What his father says is too down-to-earth and reasonable to be resisted. As a compromise, he makes it clear that he will not marry a woman who is pockmarked or has a split upper lip. On their wedding day, to his great delight, he finds his bride is neither pockmarked nor split-lipped. But it is his father, not he, who has the say about his marriage, and it is also his father who busies himself with the arrangements for the marriage with the Old Mistress of the House of Hwang, including the buying and sending of two silver rings washed with gold, and silver earrings.

Buck also describes arranged marriage in *East Wind: West Wind*, *Pavilion of Women*, *The First Wife and Other Stories*, and other novels. In so doing, she does not imply a preference for arranged marriage. It is true that before Wang Lung diverts himself in the town flower-house with Lotus, he and O-lan do live a happy life. But their happiness should not be regarded as the outcome of the arranged marriage. Instead of defending the traditional Chinese marriage system, Buck is illustrating the fruits of industry and cooperation among the Chinese farmers.

In a discussion about Buck's introduction of the elements of Chinese culture, we cannot afford to omit those in her writings about the Anti-Japanese War in China, especially as depicted in *The Patriot* and *Dragon Seed*. The two novels could be regarded as an organic whole, for they both give expression to the core values of Chinese civilization, such as responsibility over freedom, obligation over right, community over individuals, and harmony over conflict. As is well known, Chinese civilization enjoys a long history of five thousand years with continuous development, in which a comparatively stable value system is gradually formed. In her narratives about the Anti-Japanese War, Pearl S. Buck helped make better known the Chinese value system by representing what the characters say and do. In *The Patriot*, Buck describes the fighting career and personal life of Wu Yihuang in the warlord dogfight and the Anti-Japanese War. His father is a banker in Shanghai, but in spite of his affluent living he joins a young revolutionary group mainly made up of intellectuals and radical workers. When Chiang Kai-shek arrives in Shanghai and carries out a bloody suppression of dissents, Wu escapes to Japan and gets married there. But when the Anti-Japanese War breaks out, he returns to his motherland without hesitation, leaving his wife and children behind in Japan. As a Chinese, Wu holds that he has a responsibility to shoulder, and he is obliged to come back to China to take part in the resistance against Japanese invaders.

In *Dragon Seed*, Ling Tan and his family live in a small village near Nanjing: "There was nothing that he desired that he did not have. He was neither rich nor poor. . . . And thus, while they sat and while they ate together, peace filled them."[7] However, with the Japanese invasion their happy life comes to an end, and they are in great danger. Ling Tan and his villagers hate all the wars and war makers, but to fight against the increasingly atrocious Japanese army, and to defend their own homeland, they finally rise to get organized and fight in various ways with collective wisdom. For Chinese people, harmony and peace are precious, and unjust wars are hateful, but at the critical moments they meet with foreign invasions and when they are confronted with the danger of losing their homes, they will join in the collective fight, to share the national concerns, to drive out the foreign invaders, and seek revenge for their motherland. "The nation is nothing except the people and we are the people."[8] In a literary way, Buck's narratives about the Anti-Japanese War have expounded the core values of Chinese culture.

2. Interpreting Chinese Culture in Her Nonfiction

Pearl S. Buck not only introduced Chinese culture in her fiction but also interpreted it in her nonfiction by way of direct and indirect comparisons and dialogues with Western cultures. Regarding religion, one of the most important cultural aspects, Buck negated the missionary enterprise in her nonfiction and advocated dialogues. She found that in China, Confucianism, Buddhism, and Daoism exist side by side, and sometimes Chinese people believe all three, though relatively speaking Confucianism cannot be thought of as a mere religion but a philosophy, a moral guide and way of life. "A religion in the European sense of the word teaches a man to be a good *man*. But Confucianism does more than that; Confucianism teaches a man to be a good *citizen*."[9] According to Confucianism, religion is a well-ordered moral law, a high-standard way of conduct. Buck actually had a good understanding of Confucianism as an ideal of conduct. She once said, "Confucianism, which is perhaps the most complete code of personal behavior the mind of man has ever devised, was not based on any divine principle of God-giving direction, but solely on the prudent taking into account of how, given the surroundings of family and state, emperors and neighbors, rich and poor, a man should conduct himself."[10] What she said is to the point, for Confucianism became a secular religion long before she came to live in China.

However, many Western missionaries did not know much about the nature of Chinese religion, nor did they know that a system of ethics was firmly established and observed in China. As a result of their ignorance, they came to China to impose Christianity on the Chinese people, asserting that theirs was the sole God and their religion superior to that of the Chinese. Buck's parents were missionaries who came to China of their own free will, but their career as missionaries, Buck observed, was a great failure, and her mother suffered a lot. Buck witnessed and was greatly worried about the religious intolerance of most missionaries.

In *Fighting Angel*, Buck describes the tragedy of her father's life, in which he probably never succeeded in making many true converts to Christianity. And in *The Exile*, Carie is a woman exiled from God, from her motherland, and from her husband. In 1932, on a very formal occasion, Buck delivered a long speech entitled "Is There a Case for Foreign Missions?" In the speech, she answered the question with a qualified but unmistakable "no." She blamed American missionaries who were "narrow, uncharitable, unappreciative, ignorant." Talking about them, Buck told the audience: "I have seen missionaries, orthodox missionaries in good standing in the church—abominable phrase!—so lacking in sympathy for the people they were supposed to be saving, so scornful of any civilization except their own, so harsh in their judgments upon one another, so coarse and insensitive among a sensitive and cultivated people that my heart has fairly bled with shame."[11] She exposed the indifference, narrow-mindedness, and racial discrimination of American missionaries to the audience.

Buck's speech caused numerous and varied responses. Some showed their support whereas others wrote to the mission board, claiming that she should be punished. The varied responses, in fact, were a reflection of the debate over missionary activity. More and more people were opposed to the activity and began to criticize it. "Much of the opposition was grounded in recent anthropological ideas, which equated missionary activity with the destruction of foreign cultures."[12] Buck's speech is an indication of her acceptance of such tolerant anthropological ideas. With an understanding and judgment based on her observations in China, Buck saw clearly the harm that such religious imposition brought upon the indigenous religious culture. Why should the Chinese people accept Christianity when they have their own religions? Buck seemed to be challenging American mission board and missionaries to give a reply.

Buck's interpretations of Chinese culture through dialogues are represented in many of her speeches—"Is There a Case for Foreign Missions?" being only one of them. These speeches, together with some of her other nonfiction, which spans the years from the 1930s to the early 1970s, were later published under the title *China As I See It*. One of them, "The Land and the People of China," is thought-provoking because her discussion about modern Chinese democracy embodies her dialogical consciousness. She says, "when Chinese modern democracy develops, it will be in its own form, not like that of the Americans, but within its form it will contain the opportunities necessary for the life, liberty and pursuit of happiness which all people crave."[13] Her remarks are reasonable, for democracy is desirable for all, but copying others in a blind way will only bring about a harmful result to the indigenous culture. Before ending her speech, she expressed her absolute confidence in the Chinese, for in her opinion, "they have too much sense, and they are not weak, they are not decadent. China's people on the land are strong and resilient and practical. Nothing can destroy them. Only folly can ignore them, only stupidity and ignorance can despise them."[14]

It was courageous of her to have given such a positive presentation of the Chinese in 1948, just one year before the Cold War. She took the risk, on the one hand, mostly because of her understanding of the importance of the equality between different cultures in the exchange and communication; on the other hand, it was because of her understanding and love of the country she regarded as her fatherland. After she was back home and "faced with the realities of

American life," Buck "would frame China more positively through her childhood experiences."[15] To observe China at a distance and with the United States as a comparison, Buck was able to see the two countries and their cultures more clearly and arrive at more objective and convincing conclusions.

Several articles and speeches in *China As I See It* are worthy of our special attention because they focus on discussions about the necessity of mutual understanding and tolerance against prejudice and ignorance in assessing a different culture from one's own. In "China and the West," Buck traces the complex patterns of Western impact on China. In such important areas as politics, religion, literature, and aesthetics, the impact can be clearly felt. But she reminds people in the West of the great lack of understanding of China, "beyond a bit of porcelain, a painted fan, stately Mandarin figures marching across a fire screen, little was known and less cared about a country of four hundred million human beings, different in no wise in the quality of their humanity from millions of others in the globe."[16]

In the speech, Buck calls on the audience to adopt an unbiased attitude in dealing with the things concerning China and the Chinese people. Once again, she advocates the idea of "all men are brothers," and she suggests that both the Chinese and Americans "forget, for the present, country and race, and remember only that we are human beings dwelling together upon the earth, our common home." Obviously, cultural coexistence and solidarity are the essence of her suggestion. Although it is difficult for most Westerners to not look at things first from their own perspectives, it is instructive to be empathetic, that is, to put ourselves in one another's position, a position mutually beneficial for the development and progress of the respective culture.

While Western countries have their value systems and their advantages, the Chinese also have their integrity of social values and great achievements in art and philosophy. So long as contacts are established, so long as both China and the West discard prejudices against each other, peaceful coexistence will not be an illusion; after all, the Chinese and Westerners are not really as different as we have assumed. But many people believe that East and West truly are different, and they like to concentrate on the difference. In "East and West—Are We Different?," Buck analyzes the typical mentality of those who emphasize our differences:

> We like it because we like to hear of strange things, and because we enjoy the feeling of superiority it gives us when we hear that others do not have what we have, or that they do not know how to do what we do. East or West, the same look of incredulity and disappointment comes over the face of the questioner when he is given the answer, "Oh, they are very much like us—people are about the same anywhere." Something romantic, something fabulous, is gone, and we all love the romantic and fabulous. And so how alike we are![17]

Buck is being somewhat ironic in her tone here, but she goes on to suggest that we even make our villains as different as possible from ourselves. What gets us thinking is that some of us find it impossible to tolerate different customs in other cultures, yet at the same time differences are needed to enhance our sense of superiority. Buck keenly observes that "the villain in the American popular novel and movie is sly and dark and Oriental. . . . The villain in the Chinese novel or movie is tall and blue-eyed and high-nosed, with fuzzy red hair, Anglo-Saxon stature and Anglo-Saxon complexion."[18] Buck discovered a principle of selection, namely, the villain is always "the other fellow." Having lived in her several worlds, Buck witnessed a great deal of such mutual demonization.

Buck's interpretation of the Chinese novel is incorporated into her interpretation of Chinese culture in her nonfiction. During her childhood, she learned Chinese classics taught by Mr. Kung and read a number of Chinese novels. She also read many works of Western authors and was fond of those of Charles Dickens in particular. Buck not only read Chinese novels but also studied them later from an author's viewpoint; in addition, she translated into English *Shui Hu Chuan*, one of the four greatest Chinese classical novels, her title being *All Men Are Brothers* so as to make it and other Chinese novels better known in the West. Since the 1930s, she began to study Chinese novels and made speeches about them on various occasions, culminating in 1938 with "The Chinese Novel." It was the first time an author outside of China talked about the Chinese novel on such an international platform.

In the speech, she gives a vivid survey of the classical Chinese novels, including novels like *San Kuo*, or *Romance of the Three Kingdoms; Shui Hu Chuan*, or *All Men Are Brothers*, the title of her own translation; *Hong Lou Meng*, or *The Dream of the Red Chamber; Hsi Yu Chi*, or *Pilgrimage to the West; Ru Ling Wai Shi*, or *The Scholars; Yea Shou Pei Yin*, or *An Old Hermit Talks in the Sun; Ching Hua Yuen; Ching P'ing Mei*; and *Feng Shen Chuan*. It is no exaggeration to say that Buck was outlining the development and history of the classical Chinese novel.

In her studies, Buck makes historical observations on the Chinese novel, thus placing it on its own historical and cultural soil and justifying its unique though different qualities. At the same time, she makes comparative studies of the Chinese novel and its English counterpart in an empathetic way and demonstrates her *intelligence de l'autre* in her role as a cultural bridge. Her ways of introducing the Chinese novel to the world in her speeches are illuminating to the promotion of Chinese culture and literature "going global."

3. Disseminating Chinese Culture among Everyday Americans

Pearl S. Buck had a relatively in-depth familiarity with China, Chinese culture, and social reality. Although she once said that she only interpreted that part of China she knew, she regarded herself as an expert on Chinese matters. She hated books in which the Chinese people were described as strange boors, and her greatest wish was to present in her books the Chinese as they were in their real life. After 1938, by making use of her new identity as a Nobel laureate, she got involved in and organized many cross-cultural activities, and had dialogues with the Western authors preceding her so that the Chinese people in their real life and the quintessential Chinese culture could be understood.

Certainly, Buck did not make her efforts to expound Chinese culture until she was awarded the Nobel Prize in Literature. As a matter of fact, much earlier than 1938, she clearly knew the cultural prejudices and hostility between China and the United States, and she even had her personal experiences of them. As a result, she cultivated a strong sense of cultural dialogue. Once she had the opportunity, she wanted to make her attitudes clear. Among the many cross-cultural activities she got involved in and organized as a social activist, there are quite a few that have historic significance. They include the East and West Association, which she and her second husband, Richard Walsh, founded in 1941 as a vehicle of educational exchange; Welcome House, the first international, interracial adoption agency for Amerasian children in the United States; and the national campaign she and Walsh led to repeal the Chinese exclusion laws. As Michael H. Hunt remarks, Buck "devoted two decades of her adult life to trying to bring together her two childhood worlds" in order to rid the Westerners' "aloofness from China."[19] Below are some examples, from which we might have a glimpse of some of the great efforts Buck made to make Chinese culture better known to Americans.

Discovering Lin Yutang

In the field of introducing Chinese culture to the world, Lin Yutang is a very important figure, but to a great extent it is Pearl S. Buck who discovered him. Lin Yutang wrote and published *My Country and My People* in 1935, and it was well received in the United States. Lin's *The Importance of Living* (1938) created a stir and became a best seller. Afterward, the book was reprinted more than forty times; translated into over ten different languages; was sold in England, France, Germany, Italy, Japan, Denmark, Sweden, Spain, Holland, and other countries; and was influential for decades.

Moreover, Buck warmly invited Lin Yutang to go to the United States to write about Chinese culture for Western readers. In her introduction to Lin's *My Country and My People*, she writes that for a long time she had hoped that there would be a Chinese writer who would and could write a book about his or her own China, "a real book, permeated with the essential spirit of the People." When she finally was able to read such a book, she gave it loud applause. She thought, "it is the truest, the most profound, the most complete, the most important book yet written about China. And best of all, it is written by a Chinese, a modern, whose roots are firmly in the past, but whose rich flowering is in the present."[20] Buck and Lin Yutang eventually parted ways for various reasons. However, in him she had found someone who understood Chinese culture and shared her cross-cultural ideals, and who had become her strong supporter and collaborator in her efforts to bridge different cultures and to make them more familiar to everyday people. As Peter Conn rightly concludes, throughout Buck's long career, "the subject of education remained near the center of her concerns."[21] Buck's efforts in looking for allies and team members for her cross-cultural cause are illustrated in her collaboration with Lin Yutang. She realized that cross-cultural communication was no easy job, so she could not hope to do it successfully in a single-handed way.

Helping to Edit Asia

Asia, formerly *Journal of the American Asiatic Association,* was bought and renamed in 1917 by Willard Straight and aimed to introduce the colorful life of Asians to Americans so that they could become more interested in Asian people and culture. When Pearl S. Buck founded the East and West Association, *Asia* had already become the top magazine in the United States to introduce the different aspects of Asian life. But when Straight found that the number of readers did not increase greatly and therefore decided to discontinue it, Buck and her husband took over the magazine and continued to publish it for five more years until its closure in 1946.

The role that *Asia* played in matters about the Far East is immeasurable. Edgar Snow's sensational reportage, *Red Star over China*, was first serialized in *Asia* before it was published in book form; and before *Red Star over China*, the *Autobiography of Mao Tse-tong* was also published in *Asia*. Although her role as *Asia*'s president was largely ceremonial, Buck published an important statement of her editorial views. "I'm a great believer," she wrote, "in people speaking for themselves. . . . Too much is written from the outside looking in, and far from enough is written from the inside looking out. Especially is this true about the people of Asia."[22] That's why she hoped to invite Asians themselves to contribute articles that introduced their own countries and promoted their own cultures. Among the contributors for *Asia* were Jawaharlal Nehru, Lu Hsün, Mao Tse-tong, Rabindranath Tagore, Soong Ching-ling, and Hu Shih, among other world-famous figures.

Hu Shih, then Chinese ambassador to the United States, was not happy with *The Good Earth*. He said that the novel was unsatisfactory because many aspects were not reliable. However, when the news that Buck won the Nobel Prize was announced, he sent his congratulations. At the time when the Chinese people were resisting the Japanese invasion, Buck was making speeches for the Chinese and showing her support for a Sino-US alliance. In addition, the East and West Association recruited those who could speak for the Asians and invited them to come to the United States to introduce and explain their own history and civilization to American folks so that they could present their quality. The association's teaching programs also were published in *Asia*. The operation of the magazine represents Buck's great and effective efforts to put into practice her lifelong cross-cultural ideal of helping people to understand and respect cultural differences.

Founding the East and West Association

In 1941, Pearl S. Buck founded the East and West Association. In assisting with the editing of *Asia*, she realized that it was impossible for just one magazine to educate Americans, and that the best way for Americans to know and understand Chinese people and culture was to look for some Asians with a good knowledge of their own culture and civilization and an ability to describe them directly in front of Americans in the form of lectures. She understood that the relationship between two countries is based on the affection of the two countries' ordinary people, and the affection between two countries' citizens is based on the linking of their hearts. As a result, Buck found such Asians, including the Chinese, who came to the United States, and she invited them to take part in and carry out her project of cultural exchange.

Earlier on, Buck had realized that "cultural intimacy is deep understanding and close association with a physical place, region of a country, or a nation."[23] The visitors organized by the East and West Association traveled to different physical places in the United States, solo, in pairs, or in groups, to perform or to sing, all for the presentation and exchange of cultures. The Chinese among them explained to American folks the daily life, way of behavior, and spiritual pursuits of the Chinese people in a brief, vivid, and friendly way. And in their performances, they made use of traditional Chinese folk costumes, pictures, musical instruments, and operas. The visitors were chosen carefully; they were not necessarily well known and their performances were not exactly professional, but what Buck hoped to achieve was to allow the American people to have a look at Asians who were similar to them so as to shorten the distance between them. The activities not only deepened Americans' knowledge and understanding of the Chinese and Chinese culture but also helped the Asian performers become more aware of American society and culture. "It was an educational experiment, designed for friendship and mutual understanding between the peoples, especially of Asia and the United States."[24] The "educational experiment" facilitated the entry of Chinese culture into the life of American folks and improved the mutual understanding between Asians and Americans.

4. Conclusion

Michael H. Hunt argues that *The Good Earth*, "more than any other single contemporary work, shaped an American image of China."[25] I think his argument is still convincing. Buck devoted her entire life to promoting Sino-American cultural exchanges. In her fiction, she created a rich gallery of Chinese characters. In the creations with a foreign audience as the implied readers, "she explained details of life in China that a Chinese author would have considered redundant or perhaps not even consciously noticed as part of the landscape with which they were familiar."[26] As we know, those details are cultural ones about China and Chinese culture, and Buck explained those details in such a way as to "present Chinese customs as familiar, natural and correct, because so would her characters regard them."[27] Buck also introduced Chinese culture in her nonfiction—even more so than in her fiction—and disseminated Chinese culture among American everyday people. In so doing she greatly helped improve Americans' understanding of China and Chinese people and culture after they came to understand the *raison-d'être* of Chinese characteristics and values. Her multiple ways of communicating cross-culturally were most effective and are still methodologically inspiring to contemporary China, which is endeavoring to make itself better known to the world.

NOTES

1. To do translations successfully, translators usually translate works into their mother tongues rather than into foreign languages. The translation of Chinese culture and literature is no exception. Unfortunately, some of the current practices in China go against this principle because some official institutions are encouraging Chinese translators to translate Chinese works into English and other foreign languages, resulting in unsatisfying results.

2. Quoted from Liu Haiping, "Pearl S. Buck's Reception in China Reconsidered," in *The Several Worlds of Pearl S. Buck*, ed. Elizabeth J. Lipscomb, Frances E. Webb, and Peter Conn, 55–67 (Westport: Greenwood Press, 1994).
3. Paul A. Doyle, *Pearl S. Buck*, rev. ed. (Boston: Twayne, 1980), 35–36.
4. Pearl S. Buck, *The Good Earth* (New York: Pocket Books, 1939), 1.
5. Ku Hung Ming, *The Spirit of the Chinese People* (Beijing: Foreign Language Teaching and Research Press, 1978), 97–98.
6. Buck, *Good Earth*, 6.
7. Pearl S. Buck, *Dragon Seed* (New York: John Day, 1941), 9.
8. Ibid., 57.
9. Ku Hung Ming, *Spirit of the Chinese*, 28.
10. Pearl S. Buck, *China As I See It* (New York: John Day, 1970), 64.
11. Peter Conn, *Pearl S. Buck: A Cultural Biography* (New York: Cambridge University Press, 1996), 148.
12. Ibid., 149.
13. Buck, *China As I See It*, 4.
14. Ibid., 9.
15. Karen J. Leong, *The China Mystique: Pearl S. Buck, Anna May Wong, Mayling Soong, and the Transformation of American Orientalism* (Berkeley: University of California Press, 2005), 14.
16. Buck, *China As I See It*, 16.
17. Ibid., 58.
18. Ibid., 59.
19. Michael H. Hunt, "Pearl Buck—Popular Expert on China, 1931–1949," *Modern China* 3, no. 1 (1977): 35.
20. Pearl S. Buck, introduction to *My Country and My People* (Beijing: Foreign Language Teaching and Research Press, 2000), 18.
21. Peter Conn, *Pearl Buck and Education* (Perkasie, PA: Pearl S. Buck Foundation, 1992), 13.
22. Peter Conn, *Pearl S. Buck: A Cultural Biography* (New York: Cambridge University Press, 1996), 244.
23. Jeanne Stevenson-Moessner, *Portable Roots: Transplanting the Bicultural Child* (Newcastle upon Tyne: Cambridge Scholars, 2014), 76.
24. Pearl S. Buck, *My Several Worlds: A Personal Record* (New York: John Day, 1954), 357.
25. Hunt, "Popular Expert on China," 33.
26. Katrina Gulliver, *Modern Women in China and Japan: Gender, Feminism and Global Modernity between the Wars* (New York: I. B. Tauris, 2012), 26.
27. Phyllis Bentley, "The Art of Pearl S. Buck," *English Journal* 24, no. 10 (1935): 792.

CHAPTER 5

Pearl S. Buck's Promising Legacy in South Korea: The Pearl S. Buck Foundation and the Rise of Korean Multiculturalism

T. J. Park

One can hardly think of any nation that is considered more ethnically and culturally homogeneous than Korea.[1] Sometimes known to the West as a "hermit kingdom," Korea had been an exceptionally reclusive country until the late nineteenth century. Although ruled by the Japanese Empire from 1910 to 1945 and then divided into two separate states in 1948 with a Cold War rivalry in Asia between the United States and the Soviet Union, the Koreans throughout the twentieth century maintained a myth of ethnic purity as one of their national identities. However, while the northern half of Korea is still manifesting Korea's longstanding isolationism, South Korea has experimented with its version of multiculturalism since the first decade of the twenty-first century. This is a highly forward-looking venture in the context of Korean history. Interestingly, Pearl S. Buck, who got involved in Korean affairs only late in her career, was the first known person to envision the possibility of a multicultural society in Korea. Her desire to help half-American children in South Korea inspired the creation of the Pearl S. Buck Foundation (PSBF; now Pearl S. Buck International) and her vision for the social integration of mixed-blood persons in Korea and a few other Asian countries has continued through its overseas branches. This chapter will examine this relatively unknown legacy of her work in South Korea.

Pearl Buck's Multicultural Humanitarianism, 1933–47

Pearl Buck once said that she was a writer and not a humanitarian worker.[2] However, one biographer characterized her writing style as follows: "In addition to her adherence to the technique of the traditional Chinese novel, and her desire to reach the widest possible audience with her humanitarian interests, a third factor was apparently involved in Miss Buck's decision not to devote herself as fully as possible to the novel as an artistic form."[3] She indeed took her writing as a means of conveying her humanitarian messages to mass audiences across national borders. This partly explains why she gained the fame of a widely translated American writer abroad and yet gained little attention from the American literary circles. Upon her death, a *New York Times* article characterized her as a missionary of humanitarian ideals: "She was herself a missionary in the fundamental meaning of the word. Less concerned with theological orthodoxy . . . she felt it her duty in life to search out and defend the humanity common to all men: Orientals and Westerners, black Americans and children of mixed blood, the mentally retarded and the powerless."[4] She indeed conducted humanitarian works in the manner of a missionary. However, her humanitarianism had some unique qualities due to her peculiar bicultural upbringing in China.

Pearl Buck rejected the monolithic worldview held by the Christian missionary community in which she grew up. She attributed this to what she learned from her childhood Confucian tutor in China: "I became mentally bifocal, and so I learned early to understand that there is no such condition in human affairs as absolute truth. There is only truth as people see it, and truth, even in fact, may be kaleidoscopic in its variety."[5] It is no wonder that she became a multiculturalist willing to accept different and even contradictory cultural norms as equally valuable. She thus despised the parochial missionary attitude that permeated American discourses on Asian culture. Americans used to take the Christian mission in Asia as a providential outreach of their national power to Asiatic "heathens" and equate whatever converting influence, even at the destruction of Asian culture, to their goodwill toward Asians. The salvation in Asia simply meant the conversion of Asian culture to a Western one. In 1933, her criticism of this missionary bigotry caused the fundamentalists' attack on her "creedless faith."[6] This led to her break with the dogmatic wing of the missionary establishment. Although the root of her moral impulses to help the rejected and suffering ones was Christianity, she expressed her faith in American humanitarianism entirely in secular and nonsectarian terms.

Yet Buck never diminished the importance of her national identity. She saw herself as a proud American who believed in America's distinctive national culture: "I want to see my country and all other countries retain always the valuable peculiar quality which makes each one what it is, which stamps it different from every other."[7] The coexistence with other national cultures, however, would require the ending of all forms of racial and cultural bigotry. To her, America's greatest contribution to the world was not its ideological crusade but its generous humanitarian assistance. The gist of her philosophy was that Americans should be able to extend their moral sympathy for the sufferings of fellow humans to the other side of the world without seeking to impose their political or religious will. Such disinterested human influence should be America's primary mission in Asia. This idea was repeatedly expressed in her writings on the Chinese. When she became a de facto propagandist on behalf of China in the 1930s and 1940s, she argued that the Chinese, unlike the Japanese, were akin to Americans.[8] Without a propensity to demonize the Japanese, she diffused humanized images of the Chinese in an effort to arouse American sympathy with them. Her point was that the ordinary Chinese people were fellow humans just like the ordinary American people and therefore Americans should take a moral responsibility to help them as victims of aggressive war.[9]

After World War II, when she increasingly spoke on behalf of biracial children, her message was same: "I do this as an American because I believe other Americans will feel as I do when they know of the situation these children face. We are Americans and the world expects more of us than of other people."[10] Her appeal was without resorting to an ideological or religious cause. She sometimes referred to the American Constitution or Cold War imagery in order to induce popular support for her advocacy. But she rejected the kind of humanitarian mission abroad that was fueled by a desire to proselytize American culture in the name of either Christianity or democracy. To her, Asians were no less spiritual or democratic than Americans unless narrowly judged by American standards. In particular, she opposed the missionary method of using humanitarian assistance as a means of recruiting religious adherents. By appealing for the most fundamental kind of human sympathy, she tried to culturally neutralize her American mission in Asia. In doing so, she maintained an attitude of respect for contrasting cultural norms. Thus, she recognized the Asian cultural taboo against child adoption and heartily praised the Asian way of child-rearing. At the same time, however, she accepted adoption for herself and promoted it for American families.[11] Apparently, she was very much ahead of her contemporaries in appreciating the multicultural nature of the world.

Pearl Buck on Child Adoption and Amerasian Integration in Korea, 1947–65

Child adoption was at first a personal matter to Pearl Buck. She adopted children after she had undergone a hysterectomy in 1921 and her only biological child, Carol, proved to be handicapped with phenylketonuria. Her philanthropic work for "illegitimate" or mixed children started accidentally in late 1947 when an adoption agency asked her to help find adoptive families for abandoned half-Asian babies. In 1949, she launched Welcome House, the first successful private agency to break the barrier of adopting racially mixed children in America. She was also the first to raise the question of what she called "Amerasian," a racially mixed child born in Asia and fathered by an American soldier. Since many of these children were born fatherless and later abandoned by their Asian mothers, she proposed an idea to import Amerasian orphans as international adoptees for American families. This was a complicated issue. Because nationality in such Asian countries as Japan and Korea was based on patrilineal lineage, Amerasian children there were considered aliens who belonged to their American fathers. But US authorities denied any responsibility for these "G.I. babies," and immigration laws remained anti-Asian. As a result, many Amerasian children remained as "nonpersons" abandoned by both sides. Buck spoke out against this injustice. To her, it was logical for Americans to take responsibility for these children because they were half-Americans.

Of all Asian countries that hosted American troops, South Korea was probably the worst place for Amerasian children. The fatherless biracial children, whose number grew after the Korean War, were real oddities in this alleged "single-blood" nation of ultra-Confucian patriarchy. Having no patrilineal family registry (*hojeok*), Korean Amerasians had no legal identity. Also, due to their foreign features, they were uniformly stigmatized as foreign bastards born by prostitutes. Whereas the postwar Japanese government had antidiscriminatory measures for their Amerasians, the Korean government made it a de facto policy to remove Amerasians from the country by exporting them as foreign adoptees. In 1955, an Oregon farmer named Harry Holt emerged as a savior of many Amerasians in Korea. His efforts to adopt Korean orphans led to a revision of US laws that broke the barriers of a large-scale international adoption for American families. Using a method by which he served as a proxy of adoptive parents, Holt alone placed 2,420 orphans out of Korea by 1961.[12] For the next three decades, South Korea sent more than 120,000 Korean children, including thousands of Amerasians, overseas as the single biggest exporter of international adoptees. Although Buck was the first well-known person to speak for the adoption of Amerasian children, her interest in Korean Amerasians grew largely due to Holt's pioneering work in Korea.

Buck had her first visit to Korea in November 1960 at the end of her tour in Japan. Before her visit, she had requested a child welfare committee in Korea to conduct a survey of children in need of help. According to this survey, 1,518 biracial children were reported as residents in Korea, 480 of them were in childcare institutions, and 3,246 biracial children already had been sent abroad as adoptees since 1955.[13] But she believed that there were many unreported Amerasian children. During her stay in Korea, she met with Harry Holt. She had criticized Holt's proxy adoption method for being inhumane and irresponsible. And she had a problem with Holt's policy of placing children "only to people who believe in a certain Christian dogma."[14] However, she agreed that the proxy adoption was necessary given the dire situation of Amerasians in Korea. Most international observers agreed that the best way to save these poor children was to help them leave Korea as soon as possible. Some childcare workers in Korea felt uneasy about the Korean policy of exporting unwanted children overseas but offered no alternative policy.[15] Samuel Berger, US ambassador to Korea, also wrote to her: "I agree that in all probability a mixed blood Korean child is better off in the United States than he is in Korea given the present day Korean social customs."[16]

Buck yet maintained that America could adopt only a small percentage of Amerasians and most Amerasians would have to live in their land of birth. Therefore, she argued, it would be necessary to help integrate these children into Korean society. This integrationist vision became the basis of her Pearl S. Buck Foundation (PSBF), which she launched in 1964. She recalled her cause as follows:

> The fact has to be faced, however, that they are born, and that we Americans are partly responsible for them. As an American myself, I cannot believe, moreover, that it is good for American prestige for our half-American children to grow up illiterate and without the opportunity that other children even in Asia have. The result can only be a criminal class of persons of whom the Asians will say, "See what the Americans have left behind." . . . My recent visits to Asia, however, convinced me that adoption alone cannot solve the problem. We cannot at best bring more than a few children to the United States. What is to become of these half-Americans left in Asia? Can we Americans afford to let then grow up a criminal group, a constant burden in the Asian country where they happen to be born because of our military forces must be stationed there? After facing this as an American with long experience in Asia, I determined to set up a Foundation which would have my name and to which I intend to devote my own efforts for the rest of my life. Its purpose is simple. We will begin with Korea where the need is greatest. . . . The total purpose of whatever we do will be to integrate the American-Korean child into Korean society by helping him to become a good citizen in the land of his birth and therefore a benefit to his fellow citizens and not a burden and a curse.[17]

She and Theodore F. Harris, a dance instructor whom she placed in charge of administering the PSBF, justified this new mission on the ground that there might be many hidden Amerasians in Korea who would be unwilling to leave their mothers or ineligible for international adoption. They also tried to distinguish their new mission by criticizing abusive adoption methods used by international social workers and missionaries in Korea, such as forcing Korean mothers to relinquish children as orphans or obliging children to become members of the church.

Why did Pearl Buck, who knew about the unyielding Korean prejudice against mixed-blood persons (*honhyeol-in*), pursue the seemingly unrealistic goal of integration? She spared any blame on the Koreans and their culture and saw Korea's economic insecurity as a root cause of the Amerasian misfortune: "The Koreans are a kind and gentle people, civilized in heart and mind, but times are hard and orphans, Korean or half-American, are too many for accommodations."[18] Time would solve the problems of Korean prejudice. In addition to this optimism, she appeared to have sought her unique role in Korea as an international celebrity. While she visited Korea eight times throughout the 1960s and cultivated friendships with Korean notables, she sometimes took a role of spokesperson for Korea in the United States. She deplored the American people's almost zero interest in Korea and asked American leaders to express their concerns about Korea as a Cold War ally.[19] In an effort to diffuse the knowledge of Korea in the United States, she also published a historical novel on Korea in 1963 and wrote two novels about Korean Amerasians in later years.[20]

Pearl Buck's Korean Venture and the Opportunity Center in Sosa, 1965–76

In 1965, Pearl Buck and Theodore Harris launched their first pilot project overseas in Korea. Frank J. M. Davis, an assistant to them, led a project team in Korea. Unable to cover the whole country, his team conducted a case study in a G.I. camptown north of the capital city of Seoul. It identified about five hundred Amerasian children in that town, of which only one-third were registered as Korean citizens. The standards of childcare were "shockingly below even Asian standards," although such was "not a result of neglect or cruelty on the part of the Korean people." The first tasks, therefore, had to address the children's health and economic security rather than their educational opportunity or integration. Based on this study, the PSBF implemented two forms of policy in 1966. One was to find Amerasian children and get them registered by the Korean Ministry of Health and Social Affairs (MHSA) so that they could be recipients of assistance from the PSBF. The other was to organize a local project in cooperation with Korean industrialists to get the children's mothers employed in food processing plants.[21] In the United States, Buck used her celebrity status and networks to secure financial sponsors for Korean Amerasians. Her correspondence in March 1966 indicated that the PSBF mailed about twenty-three thousand letters each week to various parts of the United States.[22]

In the meantime, the PSBF secured a land property from Il-Han New (Yu Il-Han) of the Yuhan Corporation for the PSBF's first "Opportunity Center," which Pearl Buck planned to establish for Amerasian children and their mothers. New, an American-educated Korean businessman known to Buck since the years of World War II, agreed to lease his pharmaceutical plant compound in the district of Sosa (later absorbed into the city of Bucheon) near Seoul. By 1968, the PSBF had purchased this compound, which included seventy-five acres of farmland and forest, at $480,000. According to a report in April 1967, the initial cost to set up the Opportunity Center in Sosa was estimated at $1,120,000. The original plan included the facilities for childcare, medical service, vocational training, recreation, farming, and education with a dormitory for one thousand students.[23] Funding would come mostly from American sponsors. The Opportunity Center's board of directors, both American and Korean, came under a dual supervision of the

PSBF headquarters in Philadelphia and the "concerned authority" of the Korean government (MHSA). As a nonprofit organization, its prime goal was "to publicize and ameliorate the injustices, prejudices, and deprivations" on children deprived of equal opportunities, especially Amerasian children.[24] On June 11, 1967, Buck met with hundreds of Amerasian children and their mothers at an official ceremony for the Opportunity Center in Sosa. She recalled that this was the happiest day of her life.[25]

Buck was neither a trained social worker nor a passionate charity giver. She disdained the idea of offering charity "except in a temporary emergency."[26] So she styled her mission as one that offered "opportunities." She also disdained many adoption agencies as business schemes for social workers and preferred to appoint nonprofessionals like Harris as PSBF executives. Her defense of Harris's inept leadership upset many others.[27] In addition, her high-handed approach of seeking sponsors from privileged ranks of society caused what she called "jealousy" from other childcare agencies. Indeed, she considered her work in Korea as something special: "I do not want professional social workers as executives. They are excellent and necessary in certain applied areas, but I wanted and do want a new approach to Asia. I have been encouraged in this new approach by officials in the Korean government who urge us to work independently of other organizations, since we are doing something no other organization is doing, in that our sole purpose is the general welfare and education of the Amerasian child who must remain in the land of his birth."[28]

Not surprisingly, she got involved in a dispute with the Holt Adoption Agency, which criticized her integrationist policy and her condescending approach. In response, she criticized Holt's sectarian approach and insisted that the Korean government endorsed her policy because adoption agencies could place at best one-third of 1,500 estimated Amerasian children born annually.[29] The Korean government's lack of reliable data on Amerasian children helped her to justify her mission in Korea. In fact, the total estimated number of mixed-blood children in Korea varied so widely that no one was sure of it.[30]

In the end, however, Buck's distrust of professional administrators took a toll. In 1969, the Korean authority denied a license renewal for the Opportunity Center after Amerasian children staged protests against the center's mismanagement.[31] Months later, the Pennsylvania government denied a license renewal of the PSBF's fund-raising on the ground of charges of financial misuses and Harris's misconduct.[32] Although Buck was able to secure the license renewals in both cases, managerial problems continued to plague the PSBF. Stanley J. Moen, a missionary hired for directing the Korean Opportunity Center from late 1969, got involved with charges of property mismanagement and feuds with the Korean authority. Compounded with funding problems, the PSBF decided to close the center in 1971, but the decision was not executed until 1975 when M. Daniel Bailey, the PSBF's executive director then, went to Korea to release Moen from the job and settle the property dispute. According to his report to the PSBF board members, a man of racist penchant had managed the Opportunity Center in Korea without proper auditing for years.[33] Pearl Buck passed away in March 1973 without seeing this disgraceful ending of the Opportunity Center.

Despite scandals on mismanagement, the PSBF maintained a fair set of rules on funding and its contributions to Amerasian children were substantial by contemporary standards. By the mid-1970s, it had a policy to appropriate $18 per month for each child sponsored, of which $9 was granted to the child. In 1974, it sent out a total of $746,250 to its five Asian branches (Korea, Thailand, Taiwan, Okinawa, and the Philippines), of which $187,868 was for its Korean branch. Its sponsored children in Asia totaled 4,324 in 1976. The Korean Opportunity Center had twenty-two local staff members under an American director to take care of 1,172 children with a monthly budget of $14,650.[34]

The Pearl S. Buck Foundation and the US Amerasian Act of 1982

Although the PSBF's Korean branch continued to exist after the closure of the Opportunity Center in 1976, its integrationist mission lost momentum. The Korean government was ever more determined to export unwanted orphans and Amerasian children as foreign adoptees. South Korea provided over half of all international adoptees to the United States from the early 1970s.[35] In the United States, however, the aftermath of the Vietnam War raised a public awareness of G.I. babies in Asia. As early as 1968, Buck proposed a congressional hearing on Amerasians to an aide of Senator Edward M. Kennedy. By referring to the French and Dutch policies accepting biracial children from their former Asian colonies, she argued that helping these children would be a winning strategy of America's Cold War against the Communist bloc.[36] Ten years later, Kennedy led a congressional resolution to authorize two million dollars of United States Agency for International Development (USAID) funds for Amerasians through nonprofit agencies. This modest beginning of US official action for Amerasians inspired some individuals to ask for the acceptance of adult Amerasians as US immigrants. John A. Shade Jr., executive director of the PSBF, and Alfred V. Keane, a Catholic missionary of St. Vincent's Home for Amerasians in Korea, played a major role in bringing congressional attention to the Amerasian issue in the late 1970s.

In 1980, Shade published "America's Forgotten Children," the first voluminous study of Amerasian issues. In it, he characterizes the Amerasian problem as a human rights abuse resulting from US foreign policy beginning with America's first military deployment in Asia in 1898. For these neglected half-Americans, he called for "a moral commitment equivalent to that taken in behalf of the blacks" for the Civil Rights Act of 1964. Like Buck, he deplored that the American view of the world, which often lacked historical and multicultural perspectives, was a problem in understanding the

Amerasian problem.[37] The Amerasians were victims of circumstances and their misfortune was not due to the shortcomings of Asian culture in which they grew up. Asian countries were not yet ready to provide decisive help to Amerasians, and the US government—for all its capacity and proclaimed generosity—should take the initiative to help them. He thus supported an immigration bill to accept Amerasians above the age of fourteen.[38] However, in defense of the PSBF's integrationist policy, he noted that bringing Amerasians to the United States would not be the best solution because it could hurt their Asian cultural roots and cause their unwilling separation from mothers and relatives.

According to Alfred Keane, a Maryknoll missionary who took care of handicapped children in Korea, there was little or no hope of Amerasian integration in Korea. Like the late Harry Holt, Keane was a man of action. In 1977, he contacted members of the US Congress for bills designed to accept adult Amerasians as preferred immigrants.[39] Although Washington's motive to consider this issue came out of concerns about Vietnamese refugees, Keane offered examples of Amerasian life in Korea to demonstrate their desperate situations. Shade, however, objected to Keane's tactics in saving Korean Amerasians, as described dramatically in a newspaper article.[40] Like Buck, he disdained the missionary habit of exaggerating evil practices in Asia to validate their heroic efforts for salvation. His criticisms of Keane summed up the PSBF's integrationist philosophy:

> Father Keane believes that the only chance a Korean Amerasian has for a future is a one-way ticket out of Korea. We disagree. We resent those tactics he employs, for it gives us and others who address the human rights issue of the Amerasians a terrible obstacle to overcome. We dislike similar ploys set against our own operations in Korea. We do not accept that there is only one answer—adoption. We do not believe that all Amerasians should be Christian, or adopted to the U.S.A. We

> believe that adoption, or international placement, is a "selective medication" and not a "universal remedy." It is not an antidote for prejudice or condition of birth, and when it is utilized as such one simply realizes a geographical relocation of a problem, at best, and further complication of that problem, at worst. . . . The way the story is written, it would have the reader believe that Korea is a terrible place, that the Korean people are terrible people, and that the Korean government does not care—all because of the condition of the Amerasian children. That impression is untrue. . . . There is change for the better in Korea. And there is promise for still greater positive improvement for all Korean citizens, as well as the Amerasians. It is important to state this, because Father Keane's one remedy must, of logical necessity, be posited on a no-change theory. That construct simply does not hold water.[41]

Shade defended the Koreans because the PSBF in Korea in effect served as a proxy welfare agency of the Korean government when there was no official institution to take care of mixed-blood people. Its integrationist policy required cooperation with the Korean government. In the 1970s, when many Amerasians had grown older and had become ineligible for international adoption, the Korean government in fact worked with the PSBF to provide preferential treatment for them. It exempted Amerasians from compulsory military service, began providing small monetary aid, set up a vocational school for overseas job opportunities, and accepted their family registry on the maternal side by 1980.[42]

Still, the Korean government's preferred policy on Korean Amerasians was to send as many of them as possible to the United States as adoptees or immigrants, because it was considered good for them. The Koreans may have desired to remove an outcast class of foreign features for the sake of their "single-blood" nationalism. But many concerned Koreans also felt that Korean Amerasians would be much better off in the more advanced country of their fathers than in the less developed country of their mothers where opportunities were extremely limited. One common problem with Shade's integrationist agenda was that few observers expected any significant change to Korean nationalism and patriarchy in the foreseeable future. In response to the criticism that the integrationist goals would not be achieved "unless the Foundation first changes the infrastructure of Asian culture," Shade admitted that the PSBF had no right or power to change Asian society.[43]

When Shade and Keane were invited to a Senate hearing on June 21, 1982, Keane offered powerful testimonies and showed a number of letters from Korean Amerasians studying at Gonzaga University. These letters expressed their overwhelming desire to leave Korea. One letter wrote: "I do not want to remember life in Korea." Another letter wrote: "A half-American in Korea is a nobody and a nothing. We do not belong in Korea." Keane added: "They see coming to America in most cases as their only hope in life for anything." Shade, while supporting the immigration bill, held that many Amerasians would not prefer to come to the United States and therefore a better solution would be a policy to help integrate them into Korean society.[44] In fact, he knew that 89 percent of the Amerasians surveyed in a poll expressed their desire to settle in the United States. Perhaps he wanted to validate the PSBF's integrationist agenda by downplaying the obvious consensus of opinions. In any case, Congress passed the Amerasian Act and President Ronald Reagan signed it in October.

The Amerasian Act of 1982 accepted the immigration of Amerasians born in South Korea, Vietnam, Laos, Cambodia, and Thailand from 1951 to 1982 on the first category of preference. It gave truly great opportunities to thousands of Amerasians seeking to escape from their hopeless situations in Asia. Between 1984 and 1989, the Korean PSBF alone assisted 577 Amerasian youths to leave for the United States as immigrants.[45] The Korean MHSA no longer estimated the number of Amerasians in Korea after 1984 as the number was expected to decline significantly as a result of the Amerasian Act. From 1982, it had only an informal policy to distribute some financial aid from Red Cross contributions to the remaining Amerasians through the Korean PSBF. In the mid-1990s, this aid covered a monthly stipend of about forty-four dollars and tuition fees for elementary and secondary schools for each Amerasian.[46] In 1998, the Korean PSBF's role as bursar agent of the MHSA came to an end. By 1999, the Korean PSBF had only 222 children supported by American sponsors.[47] As many Korean Amerasians had already left for the United States, the PSBF's integrationist mission in Korea seemed to fade away.

The PSBI and the Rise of Korean Multiculturalism, 1999–2008

In 1999, the Korean branch of the PSBF (renamed as Pearl S. Buck International; PSBI Korea) began to provide assistance for the children of immigrants from other Asian countries who were born in Korea. South Korea had become an Organization for Economic Cooperation and Development (OECD) country where "globalization" was entertained as a media-sponsored buzzword. For its industrial demand and declining fertility rate, South Korea accepted migrant workers and brides from China and Southeast Asian countries. In particular, the Korean government helped to bring many foreign brides for Korean men in rural areas who had difficulties in finding marriage partners. As a result, the "Kosian" (Korean-Asian) families emerged as a new group of residents in Korea. These Kosian children were fathered by Korean men and thus were free from the stigma of illegitimacy. How to successfully integrate them into Korean society became a public policy concern.

In the early 2000s, PSBI Korea tried to redress the Amerasian issue in association with the Kosian issue by revealing that the life of Korean Amerasians was still extremely marginalized in contrast to the overall progress of Korean life.[48] Janet Mintzer, PSBI president and CEO since 2001, expressed her impression that "there is more discrimination against Amerasians in South Korea than anywhere else in Asia and . . . it has not improved significantly."[49] Although conveniently ignored in Korean public discourses, the Amerasian issue was increasingly recognized as a human rights issue. In 2004, the Korean National Human Rights Commission, an independent bureau created in 2001, published its first major study on camptown women and Amerasians. This study, conducted in 2003 by a human rights group called Durebang, reaffirmed the familiar cycle of low education and poverty among Korean Amerasians. Daily encounters of prejudice at school led to early school dropouts, and the subsequent lack of job skills preconditioned the life of chronic poverty. Nearly half of the forty-five persons surveyed in this study recalled their memory of attempted suicide.[50] Defining the Amerasian problem as a long neglected human rights issue, Durebang called for institutional reforms to redefine Korean nationalism and stop discrimination based on racial or ethnic origin.

In 2005, the Korean government began to consider the possibility of Korean "multiculturalism" under President Roh Moo-Hyun, a former civil rights lawyer. After reviewing the National Human Rights Commission's report, the Roh administration decided to include the issue of mixed persons and immigrants as part of its social policy agenda with a desire to overcome the old concept of single-blood nationhood.[51] Committees were set up for this task, but the Korean public remained indifferent to the debate on multiculturalism. Fortunately, the Korean authority found a potentially great source of publicity for its new policy initiative in February 2006. Hines Ward, an American football player who won the Super Bowl MVP Award, happened to be an Amerasian born in Korea. The Roh administration quickly decided to invite him to Korea with a desire to sway Korean public opinion in support of its new policy on foreigners and mixed persons.

In early April, when Ward came to Korea with his Korean mother, the Korean media celebrated him as a role model for all mixed people born in Korea. And, as one US newspaper wrote, "South

Korean media have taken up the cry to end prejudice."[52] Ward and his mother were showered with interviews and formally invited to meet President Roh. Ward also met with Janet Mintzer of the PSBI, who was also visiting Korea, and agreed to work with the PSBI for biracial Korean children. According to Mintzer, it was Ward who initiated contact with the PSBI and proposed his contribution to it. She recalls that, during Ward's visit, she was invited to a Korean congressional committee to testify on the issue of discrimination but did not yet know the Korean plan to create multicultural policies.[53] At any rate, Ward's visit proved to be a catalyst for Korea's multicultural policy initiative. Galvanizing the positive atmosphere of public opinion generated during Ward's visit, President Roh announced in April his decision to create a system of multiculturalism. Referring to the recent survey that 13.6 percent of all Korean marriages were international ones, Roh stated that the progress toward a multiracial and multicultural society is irresistible and the Koreans thus need to overcome their single-bloodline nationalism.[54] For the first time in Korea, multiculturalism became a public policy agenda.

After a two-year deliberation, the Korean Congress finally enacted the Multicultural Family Support Act in 2008, which authorized the government to stop discrimination against non-ethnic Korean settlers and to help support the successful integration of multicultural families with state-sponsored services. Although based on a Western model, this law was motivated by Korea's demographic and economic necessities rather than by the principle of cultural pluralism. Thus, its designed beneficiaries were foreign wives and their Kosian children, and its ultimate goal was to promote their conformity to the cultural norms of Korean society rather than to grant them the collective rights of minorities as in some Western countries.[55] Nevertheless, in a country where foreign-born people made up only 1.7 percent of the entire population—and many of them were ethnic Koreans of Chinese nationality—this law signified a new chapter in modern Korean history. Its continuous revisions with additional initiatives since 2008 have been impressive.

One of the bills introduced in the Korean Congress prior to the enactment of the Multicultural Family Support Act was specifically designed to redress the injustices against camptown women and their Amerasian descendants. But it was vetoed in the process on the grounds that the term "mixed-blood person" (*honhyeol-in*) was inappropriate and it would be hard to define who should be a recipient of welfare benefit because many Amerasians had already married Koreans.[56] The Multicultural Family Support Act was supposed to take care of the Amerasian issue as well. Even so, it came too late to redress the injustices against thousands of Korean Amerasians in the past. The biggest victims of prejudice in Korea for the previous sixty years were not the main beneficiaries of the new law. By 2008, PSBI Korea had become an agency working largely for Kosian families with its own budget and independent policy from the PSBI headquarters in the United States.[57] With this change, the era of supporting mixed-blood children in Korea with contributions from the United States came to an end.

Conclusion

Pearl Buck pioneered work for the social integration of racial outcasts in a country proud of its ethnic purity, which was then considered almost impossible to achieve. Although she never saw the fruits of her work, her foundation served its purpose. The Durebang study in 2003 recognized that the PSBI was the only agency supporting mixed-blood persons when there was no public institution in Korea for them. Indeed, more than 82 percent of surveyed individuals in that study responded that they had received support from the PSBI and only 4.4 percent of them responded that they ever received any government support.[58] In recognition of Buck's unique legacy in Korea, the city of Bucheon founded her memorial on the site of the Korean Opportunity Center. But her legacy should not be judged solely by the records of her foundation. Her foundation did not bring about a full integration of Korean Amerasians and did not motivate Korean policy to promote multiculturalism in 2006. After all, what she left in Korea was the vision or belief that Korea could embrace mixed-blood persons and multicultural families. She was the first and only advocate with such a belief more than half a century ago. Fortunately, this belief has gained positive momentum since 2006. Her belief along with Korean multiculturalism will be fully tested in the decades to come.

NOTES

1. Some studies ranked North Korea and South Korea as the most ethnically homogeneous countries. See James D. Fearon, "Ethnic and Cultural Diversity by Country," *Journal of Economic Growth* 8 (June 2003): 217; Max Fisher, "A Revealing Map of the World's Most and Least Ethnically Diverse Countries," *Washington Post*, May 16, 2013, https://www.washingtonpost.com/news/worldviews/wp/2013/05/16.
2. *New York Times*, March 7, 1973, 40.
3. Paul A. Doyle, *Pearl S. Buck* (New York: Twayne, 1965), 99.
4. Thomas Lask, "A Missionary Heritage," *New York Times*, March 7, 1973, 40.
5. Pearl S. Buck, *My Several Worlds* (New York: John Day, 1954), 52.
6. *New York Times*, May 28, 1933, D7; June 19, 1933, E12.
7. Theodore F. Harris, *Pearl S. Buck* (New York: John Day, 1969), 156.
8. Pearl S. Buck, "East and West—Are We Different?," speech before the Institute of Pacific Affairs, Charlottesville, VA, July 8, 1935, quoted in Pearl S. Buck, *China As I See It* (New York: John Day, 1970), 65–80.
9. Pearl S. Buck, "People in Pain," *Reader's Digest*, 39 (November 1941): 159–60.
10. Harris, *Pearl S. Buck*, 336–37.
11. Buck, *My Several Worlds*, 324–31.
12. Korean Ministry of Health and Social Affairs, "Measures for the Welfare of Mixed-Blood Children in Korea" (report at Social Work Summer School, Seoul, Korea), August 8, 1967, quoted from Arissa H. Oh, *To Save the Children of Korea* (Stanford, CA: Stanford University Press, 2015), 82. Five major adoption agencies in Korea (Child Placement Service, Holt Adoption Agency, National Catholic Welfare Conference, Seventh-Day Adventists, and International Social Service) sent out a total of 4,190 Korean children abroad, of which 2,893 were Amerasian children.
13. Minutes of the Children's Survey Committee, October 20, 1960; Hum Yun to PSB, December 23, 1960, Papers of Pearl S. Buck (hereafter Papers of PSB), Box 32, Archives of the Pearl S. Buck House, Pearl S. Buck International (hereafter PSBI Archives), Perkasie, PA.

14. Pearl S. Buck, "Unforgettable Character," undated, 1–17, Papers of PSB, Box 32, PSBI Archives.
15. Oh, *To Save the Children*, 52–56.
16. Samuel D. Berger to PSB, January 11, 1962, Papers of PSB, Box 33, PSBI Archives.
17. Pearl S. Buck with Theodore F. Harris, *The Spacious Skies* (New York: John Day, 1966), 98–100.
18. Buck, "Unforgettable Character," 7.
19. Pearl S. Buck, "Soviet Research in Korea," undated, Papers of PSB, Box 32, PSBI Archives.
20. These three novels are *The Living Reed* (1963), *Matthew, Mark, Luke and John* (1967), and *The New Year* (1968).
21. "Historical Overview of Pearl S. Buck International Inc.," undated, 36–42, Papers of Pearl S. Buck Foundation (hereafter Papers of PSBF), Box 22, PSBI Archives.
22. Buck to Mrs. Liebermann, March 10, 1966, Papers of PSB, Box 38, PSBI Archives.
23. "Pearl S. Buck Foundation, Inc. Proposed Opportunity Center," April 17, 1967, 1–8, Papers of PSBF, Box 9, PSBI Archives.
24. "By-Laws of the Opportunity Center Korea," undated (1967), Papers of PSBF, Box 9, PSBI Archives.
25. Harris, *Pearl S. Buck*, 346.
26. Ibid., 339–41.
27. Peter Conn, *Pearl S. Buck* (Cambridge: Cambridge University Press, 1996), 312, 354–58.
28. Buck to Mrs. Reierson, March 21, 1966, Papers of PSB, Box 38, PSBI Archives.
29. Buck to Mrs. Holt, March 21, 1966, Papers of PSB, Box 38, PSBI Archives.
30. The Korean MHSA counted only 1,623 registered Korean Amerasians in 1968 when the number reached its peak point. According to a *Time* magazine report in 1965, however, the total estimate reached about 20,000. In their 1966 book, Pearl Buck and Theodore Harris estimated the total number up to 50,000 based on a Korean official's letter to them. See Durebang (Korean human rights group), "Study of Human Rights Conditions of Camptown Mixed-Blood People" (기지촌 혼혈인 인권 실태조사), a report submitted to the Korean National Human Rights Commission (December 2003), 41, http://www.welfare.seoul.kr/board/download?board_num=2511&file_num=1; "Confucius' Outcasts," *Time*, December 10, 1965, 43; Buck, *Spacious Skies*, 100–102.
31. *Chosun Daily*, May 20, 1969, 6; July 27, 1969, 6; August 5, 1969, 7.
32. Donald Janson, "Buck Foundation Denied License by Pennsylvania to Seek Funds," *New York Times*, January 7, 1970, 40.
33. Bailey to PSBF board members, May 19, 1975, Papers of PSBF, Box 9, PSBI Archives.

34. "Asian Operations Fact Sheet," February 1976, Papers of PSBF, Box 9, PSBI Archives.
35. Oh, *To Save the Children*, 165–67.
36. Buck to Dunn Gifford, February 16, 1968, Papers of PSB, Box 43, PSBI Archives.
37. John A. Shade, *America's Forgotten Children* (Perkasie, PA: PSBF, 1980), 5–13.
38. Ibid., 48–55.
39. Bernard Weinraub, "A Priest's Obsession," *New York Times*, April 9, 1982, A14; Sue-Je L. Gage, "The Amerasian Problem: Blood, Duty, and Race," *International Relations* 21 (2007): 93.
40. Keane used "whatever tactics" needed to take Amerasians children away from abusive Koreans. See Mike Winerip, "Crusade and Curses of the Fair-Deal Father," *Washington Post*, December 27, 1980, B3.
41. John A. Shade, "REF: Crusades and Curses of the Fair-Deal Father," January 7, 1981, Papers of PSBF, Box 10, PSBI Archives.
42. Durebang, "Study of Human Rights Conditions," 25–35.
43. Shade, *America's Forgotten Children*, 117.
44. Hearing on "Amerasian Immigration Proposals" before the Senate Committee on the Judiciary, Ninety-Seventh Congress (June 21, 1982), 82–83, https://www.loc.gov/law/find/hearings/pdf/00139298329.pdf.
45. "Korea Program," undated, Papers of PSBF, Box 22, PSBI Archives. In 1984, the Korean MHSA estimated only 829 Amerasians staying in Korea. See Durebang, "Study of Human Rights Conditions," 41.
46. Margo Okazawa-Rey, "Amerasian Children of GI Towns: A Legacy of U.S. Militarism in South Korea," *Asian Journal of Women's Studies* 3 (1997): 88.
47. "Korea Fact Sheet," undated, 4, Papers of PSBF, Box 22, PSBI Archives.
48. Of about 4,400 PSBI-sponsored Amerasians from 1964 to 2002, 9.8 percent did not finish elementary school and 17.5 percent failed to finish middle school. Also, a PSBI survey of 673 Korean Amerasians in 2003 showed that 78 percent of them were under the absolute poverty line. See Yun-Hui Huh, "혼혈아는 서럽다" (Mixed persons are saddened), *Herald Business Daily*, April 14, 2005; Chung-Jung Kim, "어딜가도 사람대접 못받아 가슴이 아파요" (Crushed with grief because we are treated inhumanely wherever we go), *Segye Daily*, May 20, 2004.
49. Barbara Demick, "In S. Korea, a Silver Lining to Being Biracial," *Los Angeles Times*, August 6, 2004, http://articles.latimes.com/2004/aug/06/world/fg-amerasian6.
50. Durebang, "Study of Human Rights Conditions," 102.
51. Presidential Advisory Policy Planning Committee, "Participating Government Policy Report 2–30: Reinforcing Discrimination Correction" (참여정부 정책보고서 2–30: 차별시정 강화), February 2008, 172–77, Roh Moo-Hyun Archives, Seoul, South Korea, http://archives.knowhow.or.kr/policy/report/view/17213?page=4.

52. A report by Chuck Finder, *Pittsburgh Post-Gazette*, April 9, 2006, https://web.archive.org/web/2006041 1100002/http://www.post-gazette.com/pg/06099/680735-195.stm.
53. Janet Mintzer, email interview with author, May 6, 2017.
54. Jong-Heon Lee, "Analysis: S. Korea's Mixed-Race Stigma," *United Press International*, April 6, 2006, https://www.upi.com/Analysis-SKoreas-mixed-race-stigma/58921144339239; see reports in Korea's *Yonhap News, MBN News, Kookmin Daily*, and *Seoul Daily*, April 26, 2006.
55. In-Jin Yoon, "From a Migrant Integration of Distinction to a Multiculturalism of Inclusion," in *Global and Asian Perspectives on International Migration*, ed. Graziano Bettistella (Switzerland: Springer-Verlag, 2014), 103–10; Jack Jin Gary Lee and John D. Skrentny, "Korean Multiculturalism in Comparative Perspective," in *Multicultural Korea?*, ed. John Lie (Berkeley, CA: Institute of East Asian Studies, 2015), 303–24.
56. Korean National Congress's subcommittee on Women and Family, review of the "Bill on Supporting Mixed-Blood Families" (혼혈인가족지원에 관한 법률안), December 2011, 9–10, http://likms.assembly.go.kr/bill/billDetail.do?billId=PRC_X0H8G1E0W0Y9H1U3W0W9U4I1U3U3Y9&ageFrom=20&ageTo=20.
57. Since the separation in 2008, PSBI Korea has continued to remain the only major private agency supporting multicultural children in Korea. In 2016, it sponsored about 280 children with scholarships. Interview with Taek-Myung Kwon, executive director of PSBI Korea, July 26, 2016.
58. Durebang, "Study of Human Rights Conditions," 115, 125.

Chapter 6

"Always in Love with Great Ends": Pearl S. Buck on Sun Yat-sen and His Nationalist Revolution

David Gordon

The vast and ancient country of China was ready for change. The sleeping dragon, her neighbors called her, but the dragon was in trouble and waking up.

—Pearl S. Buck, *The Man Who Changed China* (1953)

Thus Pearl S. Buck frames her children's biography of Sun Yat-sen, the individual most responsible for the overthrow of China's Manchu-led Qing dynasty (1644–1912): China was a nation in distress with a seeming need for a hero (still offstage) to rush to its defense. Interestingly, scholars have yet to directly examine Buck's views of twentieth-century revolutionary Sun Yat-sen. I aim to do so here, as her evolving views on this towering figure highlight her left-leaning celebration of China's common people in the 1940s, her contrary concern to preserve elements of Chinese tradition even within what she saw as necessary change, and her cautious rightward shift in the McCarthyist 1950s. Sun's success at overthrowing the Qing dynasty and failure at establishing a replacement Chinese government reflecting his values becomes, for Buck, a lesson in the efficacy and limits of intense, artless enthusiasm to drive social change in a country as vast as China. At one point in her 1949 book *American Argument*, she confesses, "Perhaps I am always in love with great ends."[1] Buck views Sun as a personification of such great ends, even as she intermittently recognizes the various loose ends he would leave behind.

Sun Yat-sen emerged in a context that strongly influenced Buck's view of him. China's final dynasty, the Qing, featured the rule of a non-Chinese ethnic group from the north of China known as Manchus. Sun was born in 1866 into a village in the far south, a region that was often hostile toward northern China and still more hostile toward nomads hailing from north of China itself. Sun's life thereafter would fall into three broad parts: (1) growing up on China's margins and becoming a Western-style medical doctor (1866–94), (2) networking among a motley crew of potential revolutionaries to overthrow the Qing dynasty (1895–1911), and (3) working furiously to save his revolution from dictatorship and warlordism after that revolution overthrew the Qing dynasty (1912–25). As a revolutionary—and for a brief period, president of the Republic of China—Sun set forth what he termed the Three People's Principles: nationalism, democracy, and people's livelihood. Today, both the Republic of China in Taiwan and the People's Republic of China on China's mainland continue to assert their adherence to these principles, and indeed, if peaceful reunification between them takes place in the future, these principles will almost certainly play a central role. Conversely, during Sun's lifetime he was disliked by many foreigners and Chinese alike: numerous Westerners saw him as a threat to their treaty-guaranteed privileges in China, while a variety of Chinese observers viewed him as a threat to Chinese unity under other favored political figures, such as northern warlord Wu Peifu. It is clear that many vectors of the struggle to modernize China and restore its dignity flow through both Sun's life and the numerous efforts—during his career and later, and within China and abroad—to interpret his life.

To my knowledge, Buck expressed her views on Sun Yat-sen primarily in five works: (1) a 1944 didactic play called *Sun Yat-sen* that first appeared in husband John Day's *Asia and the Americas*; (2) a 1944 essay in the *New York Times Magazine*, titled "The Man Who Showed China the Vision," that accompanied the roll-out of the play; (3) *The Man Who Changed China: The Story of Sun Yat-sen,* the 1953 children's book with which I began this essay; (4) occasional remarks in essays from the 1940s that appear in her 1970 compilation *China As I See It*; and (5) certain passages from her 1954 autobiography, *My Several Worlds.* All of these sources appeared after Buck became famous, that is, after the 1931 release of *The Good Earth* and her being awarded the Nobel Prize for Literature in 1938. Accordingly, in these works she is writing for a potentially substantial audience. Let us examine each in turn.

Sun: The Play

First, there is the play titled simply *Sun Yat-sen.* This short play (fifteen pages in length) was written and performed to raise money to aid China in its struggle against Japan during World War II. In terms of content, it is more reverential toward Sun than works published later. Short scenes idealize Sun as a bold child, a patriot, a kindly doctor, a Christian, an adept fundraiser, and, above all, a man dedicated to the Chinese people. Such scenes make extensive use of melodrama. For example, the last two lines of the play as Sun lies dying are those of Sun and his final wife, Soong Ching-ling. First, Sun utters the (fictive) last words of his life: "Ching-ling—Ching-ling—never forget the people!" Next, Buck provides stage directions: "He dies and she puts down his hand gently, stands for one second looking full at the audience. The scene fades, except for her figure. She speaks to the audience." Finally, Ching-ling declares, "I never forget!"[2]

Both despite and because of its melodrama, this play was probably effective in its time and place, provided that skilled actors were used. Without the backdrop of the war and the proximity to Sun's life—he died less than twenty years previously—the play would be unlikely to engage a modern audience. Notwithstanding its shortcomings, one feature of the play that is worth underscoring is the prominence it gives to Sun's efforts to raise funds for his political causes. This was indeed an important aspect of his life's work. Nevertheless, its accentuation initially seems unusual, given the play's preference in other respects for fast-paced drama. As the play itself was intended to raise funds, perhaps the prominence it gave Sun's efforts in this regard functioned as an additional, subtle reminder to audience members to contribute to the war effort. In either case, it is a valid point regarding Sun, as he was indeed assiduous in raising money for his causes.

Sun: The Essay

Buck's essay, "The Man Who Showed China the Vision," appeared in the *New York Times Magazine* on March 12, 1944—exactly nineteen years after Sun's demise. Similar to the play—which is announced in an italicized paragraph following the article—the essay stresses the notion that Sun was a man of the people. Indeed, Buck begins with a quotation from Sun himself: "I am a coolie and the son of a coolie. . . . My sympathies have always been with the struggling people." This sets the tone for the essay as a whole, which argues regarding Sun that "he seems to have had no conception of himself. He was only the personification of a single idea, that his people ought to be free." The remainder of the essay proceeds to buttress this argument through references to various episodes in Sun's life—learning the ideal of freedom at Hawaiian schools as a teenager, being kidnapped by his country's government in London, succeeding at bringing about a revolution only to have that revolution hijacked by would-be emperor Yuan Shikai, and so forth. Despite these travails, Buck maintains, Sun's "life was really a succession of miracles" that brought him astonishing success for someone of his humble background.[3] How did he do it?

Buck stresses that in his later years, Sun "had someone very near to help him, a young, beautiful, shy girl, Soong Chingling." While her decision to marry Sun may have shocked her family, those who knew her best "speak often of her steadfast, persistent, not to say stubborn determination to do what she thinks is right." If that sounds like Buck's depiction of Sun himself, it should: "Together they [Sun and Ching-ling] made a pair whose match the world has not seen perhaps."[4] This meeting of hearts, in turn, has rendered her a fitting spiritual successor for Sun himself: "His spirit goes on. It goes on through his widow." In an apparent reference to Ching-ling's left-leaning tendencies, Buck stresses that this spirit endures, too, in "other men and women" who "work quietly and steadily, not as extremists, not as Communists, but as Chinese."[5] Thus does Sun, a figure from decades earlier in the Chinese saga, prove relevant in Buck's estimation to the mid-1940s and his nation's ongoing struggle for freedom.

Sun: The Biography

Next, let us turn to the third work, Buck's Landmark Book's children's biography titled *The Man Who Changed China*. This is where Buck expresses her views on Sun at the greatest length. The book is 181 pages long, giving Buck ample opportunity to present and comment on various aspects of Sun's activities. Even so, it is aimed at youthful readers, with the clear objective of arousing and maintaining children's interest in her main character. Accordingly, Buck might emphasize those aspects of Sun's life that she felt would interest American children, even if she as author had other views regarding what is most significant to his career. In the description that follows, I assume that the book largely reflects her actual views while remaining aware that not only her style but also the relative weighting of her themes might have differed had she written the biography for an adult audience.

From a historical standpoint, the book has a certain number of inaccuracies at the level of detail. For example, Buck claims that the revolt that led to the overthrow of the Qing dynasty began in Jiangxi province. It actually started in Hubei province.[6] She states that Sun's alias in Japan was Nakagama, whereas in fact it was Nakayama.[7] Buck also appears to have concocted a few anecdotes. For example, during the period in which Sun organized abroad against the Manchus, she places him at one point in Nanjing, where, she says, he was hiding on a boat when a man came and said he'd been offered five thousand dollars to capture him. Sun dissuades the man, who then "hanged himself for even thinking of betraying such a man as Sun Yat-sen."[8] On another occasion, according to Buck, Sun hid in a small house on the island of Hainan for six months until friends and neighbors helped him escape.[9] I have not encountered these anecdotes elsewhere. Indeed, it seems improbable that someone would hang himself for having *considered* betraying Sun (as opposed to actually betraying him), and it also seems peculiar that Sun would be present in Nanjing or Hainan—locales within China—during a period when the government had exiled him and placed a high price on his head. Overall, in cases such as these Buck appears to be exercising her creative imagination to highlight the degree of danger that Sun faced during his years on the run from the Qing dynasty.

In terms of what Buck aimed to accomplish, such inaccuracies may matter little, as other works in the Landmark biography series likewise played fast and loose with historical truth. By and large, the book does capture the flavor of Sun's life fairly well. Where it may err, broadly, is through its overwhelming stress on Sun's Western contacts and its neglect of internal dissension within the groups Sun founded and led. While Sun's Western contacts were quite important, his Japanese contacts mattered greatly as well (perhaps she steered clear of these in part because she was writing less than a decade after World War II).[10] In addition, while Buck presents Sun as almost naïvely focused on his goals, she misses the degree to which he acted as a political sharp operator working to lead organizations comprised of restive, contentious activists. Indeed, with such a backdrop of continuous infighting—particularly within the Revolutionary Alliance (1905–12)—for a larger part of his political career, it is actually noteworthy that he or his assorted followers were able to accomplish much at all, never mind spearhead a revolution against the reigning Chinese dynasty.

It is useful at this point to recall that this is a children's book, with modern juvenile literature's predilection for stories of individual triumph over adversity. Indeed, the language Buck employs is quite strong (and sometimes gendered) on Sun's individual determination, with references to him as "practical and downright, a man of action," "always dauntless," "not afraid of struggle," "refusing retreat," and so on. Regarding Sun as a child, she remarks that "Never was such a boy for climbing high to get what he wanted."[11] Moreover, as in the play and *New York Times Magazine* essay nearly a decade earlier, Sun is presented as a man of the people. Within the biography, this means that he stands in contrast to such reformers as Kang Youwei and Liang Qichao, who sought to transform the Qing dynasty into a constitutional monarchy rather than abolish it altogether. In Buck's description, they were pompous aristocrats in contrast to Sun.[12] Such a view is notable, as we will see, inasmuch as Buck will write quite differently of these reformers elsewhere.

As for the broader context in which Sun appeared, Buck summarizes it by stating, "Everything was the same and yet nothing was the same."[13] This formulation helps explain both the possibility and the necessity for a leader such as Sun: everything was the same, so China's essence remained reliably unchanged, despite which nothing was the same—and the changes had been for the worse—so China required rapid national renewal. As to what exactly had changed, Buck duly covers China's nineteenth-century circumstances: Manchu corruption ("they had grown weak and soft"), the Taiping Rebellion, the Opium Wars, the emergence of the Empress

Dowager Cixi, and the loss of the first Sino-Japanese War.[14] She also refers at one point to Sun's later attack on the fatalistic Chinese sentiment, "To know is easy but to do is hard." Interestingly, she opposes it with an alleged statement by Yen Yuan (a disciple of Confucius), "What I want is motion, activity, reality!"[15] While Yen Yuan is quite unlikely to have expressed himself in this manner, the phrasing Buck attributes to him captures the volitional outlook that she seeks to identify with Sun Yat-sen at his best.

Despite Sun's numerous desirable characteristics, in the latter part of the biography Buck expresses some doubts regarding him, rendering him in the end a flawed hero. The first doubt appears as she writes of his short period as president in 1912: "China has always reckoned time by the moon. Now, Sun decided, she was to reckon time by the sun, as the Western peoples did. All the old feast days, which the Chinese people had enjoyed for centuries, would be upset, but Sun did not care. Perhaps he did not care enough. Perhaps he had been lonely too long, and far away from the life of his own people."[16] This view correlates with a criticism she presents elsewhere, namely, that Sun was excessively influenced by his long periods of residence abroad as he organized against the Manchus.[17]

Another criticism Buck offers, both in the book and in other essays, is that Sun was better at destruction than creation. Here is a slight condensation of her expression of this in the biography: "Sun Yat-sen, while he was and will forever be an inspiration to his people, was nevertheless not a good organizer. He knew how to make people think and feel. . . . He could make them long for liberty and a better life. He could persuade them to action. But like so many other revolutionary leaders, once the revolution was over, he could not set up a sound and workable government. . . . He could overthrow, but he could not build up."[18] In her view, then, Sun had his limits and—to use a biblical metaphor that doubtless occurred to Buck herself—he could not lead his people into the promised land. Others would need to continue what he started.[19]

Sun in Buck's Essays on China

With the contents of Buck's biography of Sun Yat-sen in mind, let us turn our attention to the fourth work containing her views on Sun, namely, the essays collected in her *China As I See It*. While none of the essays in the book specifically focus on Sun, he appears fairly often in her overviews of twentieth-century China. For example, in one essay Buck states, "it is seldom the same man who can overthrow and build up again, and Sun Yat-sen's attempts to build were failures."[20] In another essay she elaborates that anti-Manchu rebels led by Sun had "found it impossible to establish a government. In the first place, they did not know how. In the second place, they had no army. In the third place, they had no money."[21] She clearly has moved far from the voluntaristic tone that prevails in her play and biography. Still another notable example of this shift appears in the following passage: "the greatest lack in the Nationalist movement was . . . something to inspire the people. . . . Even Sun Yat-sen had not been an inspiring figure. Good soul that he was, he was a plodder, not one who, if he were lifted up, would draw all men to him."[22] Much as the tone has changed, however, Buck is not simply contradicting the views she expressed in her biography. Sun had few resources, as she notes here. Moreover, he was not inspiring in a flashy way, instead earning respect through his all-too-lumbering faith in his mission (somewhat resembling her faith in her own mission). Sun certainly had great ends, but their packaging may have left a fair amount to be desired.

Sun in Buck's Autobiography

The final work providing Buck's views on Sun is her autobiography, *My Several Worlds*. Early in that work, she discusses her knowledge of Sun in the 1910s: "his name . . . I had long known, but it was always surrounded by doubt, for no one knew what to think of him."[23] It is quite plausible that members of the anxious community of foreign expatriates in China in the early 1900s viewed Sun in this manner. In contrast to Sun, Buck states, "the two men whose names were magic at this time, to me as well as to my young Chinese friends, were still K'ang Yu-wei and Liang Ch'ih-ch'ao."[24] These are the same Kang and Liang that Buck had presented negatively in her biography of Sun. The elder of the two, Kang, had written a book titled *Confucius as a Reformer,* which argued that if Confucius were alive in modern times, he would support extensive reforms in China's political system and everyday social life. Buck said that Kang "was concerned that China ought not to be a republic, and that her people were not ready for this form of government. *He was right, of course,* but unpopular, as those who are right at the wrong time always are."[25] Here it is not Sun but, rather, his political opponent Kang whom Buck praises. Surprising as this shift may be, it corresponds with Buck's overall views regarding China's modern predicament. In general, she wanted to see China modernize aggressively while maintaining as many of its traditions as feasible. On the one hand, Sun leans toward the aggressive modernization side of this formula with his insistence that China's dynastic system be abolished and replaced with a largely Western-style republic. Kang, on the other hand, manages to retain a significant measure of tradition with his notion of constitutional monarchy. For Kang, modernity enriches tradition, whereas for Sun—politically at least—modernity *replaces* tradition. We can surmise which of these Buck would ultimately prefer.

Comparing Sun and Chiang

Another way to assess Buck's views regarding Sun is to compare them with her views on Sun's successor as leader of the Nationalist Party and state, Chiang Kai-shek.[26] Chiang led the Nationalist Party and state from the mid-1920s to the mid-1970s, long after the Republic of China had moved to Taiwan. Buck's view of him tended to be negative, though often with qualifications. For example, in a

1949 *New York Times* essay included in *China As I See It*, she states that Chiang "has never quite had the courage to put his sword aside and take up the far more skillful and difficult business of serving his people." Indeed, "he was weaned on war, militarism is all he knows, and it alone he trusts."[27] This outlook accords well with her overall dim view of male dictators as expressed in her 1941 book *Of Men and Women*.[28] Moreover, in a final essay written specifically for *China As I See It*, she states that Chiang's "suspicious nature, his own limited experience, drove away from him many able and imaginative men who might have saved his government."[29] She was particularly concerned that the ultrarich relatives of Chiang's wife, Soong Mei-ling, pulled him far in the direction of excessive Westernization and financial corruption.[30]

How do these opinions accord with her views of Sun? In her 1944 play and essay, she pointedly refused to mention Chiang's name even as she extolled Soong Ching-ling. We see this in the play's final scene, in which (as quoted earlier) Sun's final words, directed to Ching-ling, are that she must never forget the people, and she declares that she will never forget. By 1944 when the play was written, Soong Ching-ling had adopted a largely pro-Soviet outlook, thereby placing herself considerably to the left of where Sun stood at the end of his life. Meanwhile, Ching-ling's sister, Soong Meiling, had helped cement Chiang's move substantially to the *right* of Sun's center-left standpoint. By omitting both Chiang and Soong Mei-ling, even as the Western Allied powers of World War II had aligned themselves with Nationalist China, Buck is strongly indicating her preference for a leftward interpretation of Sun's legacy.[31]

So far, so progressive. Would her Landmark biography, written in 1953 after the Communist revolution, present a similar perspective? In the latter part of this longer work, Chiang appears fairly often. Here, however, the references to him are uniformly positive. Indeed, Buck contrasts Chiang's realistic assessments of people around Sun with Sun's own overpositive assessments. For example, in the early 1920s an erstwhile ally, warlord Chen Jiongming, turned against Sun. Buck states that "Chiang Kai-shek had warned Sun Yat-sen that General Chen could not be trusted, but Sun had not heeded the warning. Chiang was right."[32] Later, Sun entered a tactical alliance with the Soviet Union, inviting Soviet advisor Mikhail Borodin to his power base in Guangzhou. Buck states that years afterward Chiang "became alarmed at Borodin's power . . . and alarmed, too, at the influence he had over Madame Sun Yat-sen"—Madame Sun Yat-sen being none other Soong Ching-ling![33] Furthermore, as Sun is on his deathbed, Buck has him receive a telegram reassuring him that "General Chiang Kai-shek had matters well in hand" down in Guangzhou.[34] Either sincerely or out of a sense of fear, Buck decided in that McCarthyist period to write warmly of Chiang, whom most Americans had come to view as the leader of "Free China" in opposition to the newly established Communist "Red China."

Conclusion

In sum, Buck's views of Sun Yat-sen were in flux as, on various occasions, she cast her eye back on his legacy. For the most part, she saw him as a hero—in her terminology, a dauntless, remarkable man. Despite this inclination, she wrote forthrightly of such shortcomings she espied as an excessively Westernized outlook, a deficit in organizational skills, and a certain naïveté in his dealings with other people. In her view, Chiang Kai-shek was a more realistic figure. Chiang, however, was so wedded to militaristic means that he tended to lose sight of any idealistic ends at all. As Buck herself was "always in love with great ends," this would cause the scales of her judgment to tip, overall, in favor of Sun Yat-sen.

NOTES

1. Pearl S. Buck, *American Argument*, with Elanda Goode Robeson (New York: John Day, 1949), 203.
2. Pearl S. Buck, *Sun Yat-sen: A Play* (London: Morrison and Gibb, 1944), 32.

3. All quotations in this paragraph appear in Pearl S. Buck, "The Man Who Showed China the Vision," *New York Times Magazine*, March 12, 1944, 9.
4. Ibid.
5. Ibid., 35.
6. Pearl Buck, *The Man Who Changed China: The Story of Sun Yat-sen* (New York: Random House, 1953), 114.
7. Ibid., 84. Nakayama is a common Japanese name that, pronounced in Chinese as Zhongshan, became the main name by which Sun was subsequently known in China.
8. Ibid., 65.
9. Ibid.
10. E.g., Buck placed special emphasis on Sun's American advisor, Homer Lea (see Buck, *Man Who Changed China*, chapter 7, "The Hunchback"), while omitting any mention of Miyazaki Toten, a follower who provided him access to several prominent Japanese politicians.
11. Buck, *Man Who Changed China,* 88, 103, 122, 169, 9.
12. See, e.g., ibid., 87–88.
13. Ibid., 3.
14. Ibid., 4–5, 35–36. The quotation regarding Manchus appears on page 4.
15. Ibid., 41.
16. Ibid., 127.
17. See Peter Conn, *Pearl S. Buck: A Cultural Biography* (Cambridge: Cambridge University Press, 1996), 54.
18. Buck, *Man Who Changed China,* 144.
19. The poignantly unfinished character of Sun's revolution is stressed near the end of Buck's play (*Sun Yat-sen,* 30, 31).
20. Pearl S. Buck, *China As I See It*, comp. and ed. Theodore F. Harris (New York: John Day, 1970), 205–6.
21. Ibid., 282.
22. Ibid., 289.
23. Pearl S. Buck, *My Several Worlds: A Personal Record* (New York: John Day, 1954), 103.
24. Ibid., 121.
25. Ibid.; emphasis added.
26. Chiang's name in much English-language literature is a Cantonese rendering. In Mandarin Chinese, it is written in pinyin spelling as Jiang Jieshi.
27. Buck, *China As I See It,* 258.
28. Pearl S. Buck, *Of Men and Women* (New York: John Day, 1941). See especially chapter 7, "Women and War."
29. Buck, *China As I See It,* 286.
30. See, e.g., Michael H. Hunt, "Pearl Buck—Popular Expert on China, 1931–1949," *Modern China* 3, no. 1 (January 1977): 42.
31. Buck biographer Peter Conn points out that on March 12, 1944, Buck

held a rally at the Metropolitan Opera House to commemorate the anniversary of Sun's demise. Her speech on that occasion praised Sun while linking him with Soong Ching-ling and omitting any reference to Chiang Kai-shek. Buck's play, likewise written in early 1944, appears to adopt a very similar standpoint. Conn, *Pearl S. Buck,* 280.

32. Buck, *Man Who Changed China,* 160.
33. Ibid., 169–70.
34. Ibid., 177.

CHAPTER 7

China's Recent Realization: The Real Peasant Life Portrayed by Pearl S. Buck

Kang Liao

Many scholars, American and Chinese alike, have asked me these questions: "Why do we still read Pearl S. Buck today? After all, she was an American. Did she know the Chinese peasant life better than Chinese writers do? Are her novels more valuable in any way than the books of her contemporary Chinese writers? Even though she opened the eyes of Westerners to the life of the majority of Chinese people, what is the significance of studying Buck now for the Chinese people themselves?" Even Lu Xun, the greatest Chinese man of letters in the twentieth century, assumed in his letter to Yao Ker on November 15, 1933, "It is always better for Chinese to write about Chinese subject matters, as that is the only way to get to the truth. It is no exception even with someone like Mrs. Buck, who was warmly welcomed in Shanghai, and who regards China as her own motherland. Her books after all reveal no more than the position of an American woman missionary who happens to have grown up in China. . . . Only when we Chinese begin to do it, can some truth be revealed."[1] As we can see, Lu Xun's dismissal of Buck was goaded by national pride, which was a natural reaction to the imperial oppression that China had suffered up to that time. Under those circumstances, Chinese scholars would have a difficult time making a fair evaluation of her work. Only recently, after the Cultural Revolution ended, did we abandon the red glasses tinted with Communist ideology, and many social and historical studies of the lives of Chinese peasants in the past were conducted. Then Chinese scholars began to realize that Buck was not only the first to write about China's peasants—the first not just in the United States but in the world—but also the first to see the relationship between Chinese peasants and landlords truthfully and to write about it realistically. Moreover, Chinese scholars realized how important it is to see the truth and present it in literature after we learned what disastrous consequences the lies had caused. This essay demonstrates how this realization was achieved through a brief historical review that emphasizes a political current in modern Chinese literature.

Just like traditional European literature before the nineteenth century, China's is also all about royalty and aristocrats, as well as scholars and outlaws. Throughout China's literature of three thousand years or so, the classical Chinese poems are short and mainly about emotions and ideas. There are very few long narrative poems and no epics; stories and novels are about strange happenings, affairs of state, and the lives of noble men and women. They do not cover ordinary life, and certainly none are about peasants. Their life was boring—or so the writers thought. In discussing the significance of Lu Xun's literary works in the history of Chinese literature, Xiuji Huang made the following statement:

> For thousands of years in ancient agricultural China the position of peasants was the lowest, and therefore, they were never portrayed in classical Chinese literature except some poems that pitied them. Although *Shui Hu Zhuan* is about the peasants' uprisings, yet the genuine peasants who are engaged in agricultural work are few in the novel. . . . It was not until after the May Fourth New Cultural Movement that Chinese peasants became the major subject represented in literary works.

> And Lu Xun was the first writer in the history of Chinese literature to describe ordinary peasants.[2]

Indeed, Lu Xun was the first important author of essays and stories about ordinary people, but he didn't write a novel. Even in his famous short stories "The True Story of Ah Q" (鲁迅: 阿Q正传, 1918) and "The New Year's Sacrifice" (祝福, 1926), the protagonists are not peasants. Ah Q is a village lout who does odd jobs from time to time, and Mrs. Xianglin is a nanny and domestic helper in a rich man's house. Then Pearl Buck's most famous novel, *The Good Earth,* was published in 1931 and it immediately became a very popular and influential novel about Chinese peasant life. However, it is hard to claim its influence on the ensuing novels by Chinese writers about life in the countryside because they had their national pride and would not admit it. More important, their novels are very different from *The Good Earth*. Mao Dun's countryside trilogy (茅盾: 春蚕, 秋收, 残冬, 1932–33), Wang Tongzhao's *Mountain Rain* (王统照: 山雨, 1933), and Xiao Jun's *Village in August* (萧军: 八月的乡村, 1935) are the predecessors of proletarian revolutionary literature. Xiao Hong's *Stories of the Hulan River* (萧红: 呼兰河传, 1940) are typical local color writings and their literary value is much greater than any of the other three books, but unfortunately the writer died too young, and her style was soon replaced by that of the proletarian revolutionary literature.

The so-called proletarian revolutionary literature developed under the guidance of Mao's "Talks at the Yan'an Forum on Literature and Art" (毛泽东: 在延安文艺座谈会上的讲话), delivered and published in 1942. These talks influenced China's literature in the twentieth century more than anything else and the influence, though dwindled, can still be felt today and may even be reviving. The main point of the talks is that, although art and literature have their own characteristics and must follow their own rules in their development, they are, after all, political tools, tools of the revolutionary cause, which was to fight against imperialism and the exploiting class. Art and literature must serve the masses, the workers and peasants, and educate them as well as the artists and writers themselves. Mao's talks were thus the manifesto of the proletarian revolutionary arts and literature that particularly encouraged the writing of peasants, for peasants, and even by peasants.

Under Mao's guidance, artists and writers went to villages to experience what peasant life was like and to gather material for their artistic and literary creations. This was a good thing, but they stayed in the countryside for only a few months, or a couple of years at the longest, certainly not like Buck, who lived among Chinese peasants for decades. What is worse about the works of these revolutionary artists and writers is that they were tools to serve a political cause, and therefore they had to be politically corrected and perfected. Take the collectively created opera *The White-Haired Girl* (白毛女), for example; the original true story is that a country girl who worked in a landlord's house as a domestic helper was seduced by the landlord, who would not marry her. She could not bear the shame, ran away, and lived in a mountain alone for years. Her hair turned gray for lack of salt and sunshine, and she was thought to be a ghost because she was spotted several times when she went to steal the offerings in the local temple at night. When the Communists came, she was saved.

To emphasize the class hatred and struggle, the storyline was "improved" like this: The girl's father owes the landlord some money and can't pay him back. The landlord presses him so hard that he sells his daughter to the landlord as a bondmaid and then commits suicide. The landlord rapes the girl. The girl runs away but keeps herself alive by her hatred and determination for revenge. She once scares the landlord half to death in the temple, and eventually avenges herself and her father when the Communist army liberates the village. Musically the opera is a harmonious combination of Western opera and Chinese national music and folk songs. The opera was an instant success, but in order to make it more revolutionary, it underwent further revisions guided by Mao's talks. For instance, the girl was not sold to the landlord but taken away by force, and her father fought the landlord to death. Her hope to marry the landlord was cut out and later another character was created, the girl's fiancé, who gave the landlord a good beating, escaped to join the Red Army, and eventually returned to the village to lead the fight against the landlord class. The opera became the most popular theatrical product in the Communist areas of China. The audience's appreciation was much more than artistic catharsis. They were incited to fight the landlords in their villages. Some bourgeois intellectuals wrote articles to describe the revolutionary baptism they experienced seeing the opera and the awakening to class-consciousness the opera brought about.[3]

If the opera only praised the new Communist society and awakened the audience's class-consciousness, Zhou Lipo's *Storm* (周立波: 暴风骤雨, 1948) and Ding Ling's *The Sun Shines upon the Sanggan River* (丁玲: 太阳照在桑干河上, 1948) taught readers and communist leaders how to incite peasants' hatred for landlords and how to carry out the class struggle in the country. These two novels are the best of China's proletarian revolutionary literature, and the latter also won the Stalin Prize for literature in 1951 for its revolutionary value and functions.

The novel *Storm* is a literary illustration of the revolutionary policy and method of the Chinese Communist Party during the land reform movement. It demonstrates how the peasants are made to realize that the landlord exploits them, to awaken to the so-called truth that the landlord class is their enemy, and only by overthrowing it can they ever live a decent life. The peasants' hatred for the landlord is incited, and they are mobilized and organized to fight the enemy. The revolutionary storm breaks down the old productive relationship that has existed for thousands of years. The peasants gain the courage to take the landlord's property and divide the land among themselves. The landlord is beaten up, conquered, and killed. The novel is full of such violence and violent language, and worst of all, such violence is justified by the class struggle theory that permeates the novel.

Similarly, *The Sun Shines upon the Sanggan River* also celebrates revolutionary violence. This novel describes the relationship of people in the country as nothing but landlord versus peasants, with class oppression by the landlord and struggles against him by the peasants. The landlord in this novel lets his son join the Communist army to protect his class interests. He makes his daughter marry a Communist to corrupt the key leader of the new power. He also encourages his niece to have an affair with a peasant leader in order to set up a sex trap. The peasants in the novel are taught by the Communists to rise against the landlord. Everyone is shown as being a tool of class struggle, and the peasants' victory in the struggle is demonstrated as the sole drive of historic progress and agricultural productivity. Hatred, cruel revenge, and even killing are illustrated, rationalized, and revered as the indispensable sacrificial ritual of the revolution that will supposedly improve most people's lives.

These novels, among many others, are not without a certain artistic achievement. Like the opera, they vividly portray some peasants, farmers, and landlords; poignantly describe their psychological activities as well as their daily lives; and successfully use their language in speech representation along with the authors' own language for narration. However, the authors used class struggle as the key in these novels that aimed at serving the proletarian politics. They made their novels literally the revolutionary manuals for other Communists to follow in the land reform. These novels became the models of China's proletarian literature for later writers to imitate. As a result, at least a million landlords and rich farmers were physically eliminated, and many more were persecuted or reduced to utter destitution, and even their children were made to pay for their parents' "debts" and to suffer for their parents' "crimes."

China's land reform was the single most important reason that the Chinese Communist Party led by Mao defeated the Nationalist

Party under Chiang Kai-shek. Many people wondered how the Chinese Communist army with weapons no better than rifles could defeat the Nationalist army equipped and financially supported by the United States and with captured and surrendered weaponry and ammunitions from the Japanese troops at the end of World War II. Many Taiwanese students explained the stunning loss in the following manner: the Communist soldiers forced the Nationalist captives to charge at the very front, and their brothers, of course, would not shoot at them. That was what the Nationalist authorities taught them in school. Some Chinese lovers of the military say the Nationalist army was defeated because the Communist army had a great general, Lin Biao. That makes somewhat better sense, and Lin Biao was indeed an invincible military strategist, one of the best in China's history. But we know that a war is never won by one man. If we had to choose one man for the Chinese Communist victory, it would have to be Mao, who found the right way. The right way is not always the moral way. In fact, it is more often than not the amoral way as discussed in *The Prince* by Machiavelli. In this case, the Communist victory was won through land reform as Mao stated in *On Coalition Government* on April 24, 1945, "In order to defeat Japanese invaders and build a new China, we must conduct the land reform and liberate the peasants."

The first wave of the land reform started in 1946, three years before the People's Republic of China was founded. It was conducted in the Communist areas of China, mainly in the north, and it won the party millions of supporters among the poor and middle peasantry. This happened because the land and other property of landlords were expropriated and redistributed so that each household in a rural village would have a comparable holding. This Communist practice seemingly embodied the Confucian ideas of 均富 (equal wealth) and 不患贫, 患不均 (Do not worry about poverty, worry about unequal distribution of wealth). These ideas are epitomized by the slogan 耕者有其田 (Those who plough the field should have their own land), and it has been the dream of a perfect world that China has endeavored to realize for more than two thousand years. The question is how. In China it is always by violence. Throughout the two thousand years since these ideas were raised, in every peasants' uprising, the rebels used this slogan, grabbed the land from the rich, and gave it to the poor. Thus, they won the support of the poor who were many and defeated the rich who were few. What the Communists did was no exception, as they acknowledged: "The making and implementation of *The Outlines of China's Land Law* of 1947 abolished the feudal land system in the liberated northern areas of 160 million people, providing the liberation war with political, economic, and military resources. Therefore, the land reform has an important historic significance."[4]

This agrarian revolution was made infamous in the West by William Hinton's book *Fanshen*, which can be translated to *Stand Up*. Ren Bishi, a member of the Chinese Communist Party's Central Committee, stated in a 1948 speech: "Thirty million landlords and rich farmers would have to be destroyed," and Mao himself estimated that only 800,000 landlords were killed.[5] Mao insisted that the people themselves, not the security organs, should become involved in killing the landlords who had oppressed them.[6] This was quite different from Soviet practice, in which the counter-revolutionaries were arrested and secretly executed and often buried before sunrise. Mao thought that peasants who killed landlords with their own hands would become permanently linked to the revolutionary process in a way that passive spectators could not be. Actual numbers killed in the land reform are believed to rank in the millions, as there was a policy to select "at least one landlord, and usually several, in virtually every village for public execution."[7] In 1976 the US State Department estimated that there may have been a million killed in the land reform.[8]

What was a landlord? What was a rich farmer? By the Communist definition, a landlord was a farmer who had enough land to live on and did not need to work the field but hired hands to work for him or practiced usury. A rich farmer was one who had land and worked the field but also rented his land to peasants or practiced usury. To become landlords or rich farmers was the dream of most peasants. They might be jealous of landlords and rich farmers, but they found nothing wrong in being them. There was little so-called class hatred or class struggle. Therefore, in the land reform, the major task of the Communist work team was to make peasants understand that landlords and rich farmers preyed on them and exploited them. They helped peasants recall and understand the crimes of landlords and rich farmers. They incited class hatred toward landlords and rich farmers, mobilized and organized peasants to fight them, take their land and property, and even eliminate them if they were not subdued.

Such fights were described in novels like Zhou Lipo's *Storm* and Ding Ling's *The Sun Shines upon the Sanggan River.* There is nothing wrong in describing the struggle and the process of land reform truthfully, but the problem is in the attitudes of the authors of those literary works. They justified the cruel class struggle and taught many Communists how it should be conducted. They not only served the Communist propaganda in land reform but also set vivid examples of how to do it for some backward areas and for the second wave of land reform all over China from the mid-1950s to the end of 1952. We can see the formula in those novels: (1) they describe exploitations and oppressions by landlords and rich farmers; (2) they incite hatred between peasants, rich farmers, and landlords; (3) they educate peasants and mobilize them in the struggle for their liberation; (4) they show the struggle as part of the proletarian revolution in the whole country and even part of the international anti-imperialism campaign; (5) the communists expropriate the land and property of landlords and rich farmers and redistribute them among peasants; (6) fights between the classes follow and always end with the peasants' triumph. This is how the East was won, and the proletarian literature played an indispensable role in the victory.

The violation of the sanctity of private property and the democide of at least a million landlords and rich farmers were the original crimes of the Communists. However, such injustice committed in land reform was justified by the media of Communist propaganda as well as the Chinese literature from the 1950s to 1970s, including Liang Bin's trilogy, *The Saga of the Red Flag* (梁斌: 红旗谱, 播火记, 烽烟图, 1958–83) and Hao Ran's two series of novels: *The Bright Sunny Day* and *The Golden Broadway* (浩然: 艳阳天, 1962–65; 金光大道, 1972–77). These novels again and again use class struggle as the theme, portray peasants and landlords as class enemies, and advocate and glorify violence against the class enemy in the name of revolution. These novels do not lack charm, but their charm did more harm than Plato and Confucius ever feared literature could do to society and human beings. Two generations were affected by the proletarian revolutionary literature ever since Mao published his talks in 1942. Chinese readers were enchanted by the descriptions of the poor peasants' sufferings, by the portrayals of the hateful class enemies, and by the exciting class struggles in those novels. Their class hatred was stirred and directed at landlords and later at intellectuals, as most of them were the landlords' descendants. Their class love was aroused and directed to the Communist Party and the leaders and eventually to Mao alone. Humanism was replaced by the theory of class struggle, against which everyone and everything was measured. Spouses condemned each other. Children exposed their parents' counter-revolutionary crimes. Communists fought Communists. Young students sacrificed their lives trying to save a few desks and chairs from fire or flood because they were the property of the proletarian state, but no one would try to save a drowning man because he might be a counter-revolutionary criminal committing suicide. Immanuel Kant's categorical imperative was "rightfully" disobeyed in China during the Cultural Revolution.

It's not really hard to see how all this could happen. The chain of logic is actually quite clear. Private property is evil. The more property one has, the more evil one is, and so his property must be taken away and redistributed to others. Now he is less evil, but everyone else is a little more evil than before, and so in a perfect world all property must be taken away by the state, and we all work together selflessly for the common good. The trouble is there are always some officials in charge of distributing property in the state, and a new class enemy is bound to emerge even among the Communists themselves. Therefore, continuous revolution is a necessity, as Mao said in a letter to his wife Jiang Qing on July 8, 1966: a revolution must be made "once every seven or eight years."[9]

After the Cultural Revolution, in which not only Chinese intellectuals but also almost all Communist leaders were persecuted by turns, the Chinese people awakened to the impossibility of Communism and to the harm of the class struggle theory. They realized that the vicious cycle of continuous fights began with the wrong presupposition that private property was evil. Under Deng Xiaoping's influence, the Communique of the Third Plenum of the Eleventh Party Congress stated in 1979 that "large-scale turbulent class struggles of a mass character have in the main come to an end," and Deng flatly ruled out the possibility that a new exploiting class could emerge under the socialist mode of production.[10] The Communist leaders realized that private property was not evil. It was good and its sanctity must be held in awe and protected by law. Their children quickly divided the state property among themselves and happily became new capitalists or landlords, except that they don't call themselves that. They are called industrialists or land developers. But Chinese people began to challenge the literary theory that maintains, on the one hand, as Mao advocated, that art and literature must serve the proletarian revolutionary cause, and, on the other hand, asserts that art and literature should disregard truth, as Vladimir Nabokov expressed in a metaphor, "The magic of art was in the shadow of the wolf that the boy deliberately invented, his dream of the wolf; then the story of his tricks made a good story."[11] Chinese people have seen that the damage of the dream of the wolf was much greater than the loss of a few sheep.

They know what terrible consequences could result from the tantalizing world created by the magic of artistic writers, if they were also political fanatics.

The Chinese people have realized that only in a free and democratic country can people afford to enjoy art for art's sake, but today's artists in China still have a solemn duty of describing life as it is. And to learn a history lesson, they still need to describe life as it was. What was life really like in the old society before the Communists took power? What was the relationship between a landlord and peasants? Did a peasant ever become rich under the landlord's oppression and exploitation? If so, how? Our Confucian scholars despised peasants, and no one found their lives interesting enough to write about. Our Communist writers distorted the relationship between a landlord and peasants with the class struggle theory and political agenda. Some old people still remember, and what they told us we found strikingly similar to what we read in Pearl S. Buck's novels. The conflicts in *The Good Earth*, for example, are between man and nature, man and woman, men and other men, and even among one's own family members like Wang Lung and his uncle—individuals, not classes. The conflicts can be between a woman and other women, or in one's own heart, internally, mind and body, different desires. A landlord does not always remain rich, like Hwang, who sells his land to Wang and gradually becomes poor, whereas Wang Lung becomes rich through hard work and frugal living and with a little bit of luck. The relationship between a landlord and tenants can be friendly like that between Wang Lung and Ching. People from different classes are not necessarily enemies, but they may need one another and even love one another. The ruling class fight among themselves for power and dominance more ferociously than they oppress the working class, which they need to use rather than kill.

These truths are so simple that they are taken for granted in the West, but they were surprising to the Chinese people, who were brainwashed with the Communist class struggle theory. Chinese readers saw a completely different world in Pearl S. Buck's novels, a much more believable world of China's countryside and peasant life. After the Cultural Revolution, Chinese writers also began to publish works that are different from the mainstream of the proletarian revolutionary literature, and their works have quickly become the mainstream. Their works echo, enrich, and reinforce Buck's portrayal of Chinese peasants and farmers. They all demonstrate far fewer and less severe class conflicts between peasants and landlords or rich farmers. They all depict more conflicts between man and nature, peasants and wars or political movements. They all reveal conflicts caused by the farmers' dreams, desires, jealousy, or greed. They show peasants' conflicts with bureaucracy, regulations, and officials. They also illustrate conflicts between traditions and new ideas. In a word, we find more and more similarities to Buck's novels in post–Cultural Revolution Chinese literature about China's peasant life. Some of these writers, like Zhou Keqin (周克芹) and Chen Zhongshi (陈忠实), have gained national fame in China. Mo Yan (莫言) even won the most famous international prize, the Nobel Prize in Literature in 2012. And yet, I want to mention a writer that most people may never have heard of, Xie Baoyu (谢宝瑜), who published only one novel, *Rose Valley* (玫瑰坝, 2006). This book vividly shows the vicissitudes of a mountainous village in Sichuan province of China and demonstrates the catastrophes the land reform brings to the peasants and farmers there. The novel portrays some vivid characters and through their tragedies reveals the darkest hue of human hearts when conditions allow evil to prevail. This novel is not widely accessible in mainland China yet, but I believe it will stand side by side with *The Gulag Archipelago* by Aleksandr Solzhenitsyn.

There is, however, one obvious difference between all these realistic novels of much later Chinese writers and Buck's novels about the Chinese peasants' life in the past, and that is a certain legendary color, which is particularly evident in her peer laureate Mo Yan's novels. After all, these writers only heard of or imagined the stories they wrote but did not experience them. Therefore, we cherish Buck's realistic works because she was there, saw the lives of Chinese peasants, knew their language, and had a way of writing their stories artistically without any ideological prejudice or political purpose.

As we can see, the Chinese writers from the Confucian era to the first thirty years of the Communist regime missed the boat on Chinese peasant life for different reasons. For the Confucian intellectuals, the peasants occupied an unimportant place in the society and ideology. The Chinese examination system offered men only one social ladder, and that was to study and test into officialdom. This system believed in a hierarchy based on gender and educational levels. With such priorities, it lacked sympathy for the uneducated peasants who were supposed to occupy a low rung on the hierarchy. The Communist writers, conversely, seeing the peasant's misery as an engine of revolution, were encouraged to use the peasants for political gains. Neither of these types of writers described the peasants' daily life, struggles, aspirations, and values truthfully. The Confucian writers ignored peasants with only the exception of a few poems that pitied them. The Communist writers distorted peasant life. It was not until Pearl S. Buck that Chinese peasant life was described realistically and accurately. For this reason, we should acknowledge her as the most important literary figure and perhaps even the "mother" of describing the life of the Chinese peasant.

NOTES

1. Yao Hsih-pei, "What Pearl Buck Said about Lu Xun," *Lun Xun Monthly* 6 (1990); translation mine.
2. Xiuji Huang, *A Concise History of Contemporary Chinese Literature* (Beijing: Chinese Youth Press, 1984), 59; translation mine.
3. For details of the creation, revision, and reviews of the opera *White-Haired Girl*, see Tang Tao and Yan Jiayan, *A History of Contemporary Chinese Literature, vol. 3* (Beijing: People's Literature Press, 1985), 259–69.
4. Zhao Lan, "The Exposition of a Historical File, *The Outlines of China's*

Land Law," Chinese Treatise website, http://www.xzbu.com/4/view-1621535.htm; translation mine.

5. Rudolph J. Rummel, *China's Bloody Century: Genocide and Mass Murder since 1900 (New Brunswick, NJ: Transaction, 1991),* 223.
6. Philip Short, *Mao: A Life* (New York: Holt Paperbacks, 1999), 436, 437.
7. Denis Twitchett, John K. Fairbank, and Roderick MacFarquhar, *The Cambridge History of China (Cambridge: Cambridge University Press, 1978).*
8. Stephen Rosskamm Shalom, *Deaths in China Due to Communism* (Tempe, AZ: Center for Asian Studies Arizona State University, 1984), 24.
9. Mao Tse-tong, "A Letter to Jiang Qing on July 8, 1966," Education on Literature, History, and Philosophy, October 2004, http://www.yxjedu.com/li_shi_shun_jian/lishi_shunjian_lan_mu/mao_jiang_xin.html.
10. Deng Xiaoping, "Uphold the Four Cardinal Principles," March 30, 1979, *Selected Works* (Beijing: Foreign Language Press, 1984), 176.
11. Vladimir Nabokov, "Good Readers and Good Writings," in *The Norton Reader: An Anthology of Expository Prose, 9th ed., ed. Joan Hartman,* John C. Brereton, and Linda H. Peterson (New York: Norton, 1996).

Chapter 8

Gateways into *The Good Earth*: Myth, Archetype, and Symbol in Pearl S. Buck's Classic Novel

Carol Breslin

Pearl Buck's prize-winning novel *The Good Earth* is an acknowledged classic of twentieth-century literature. Now, over eight decades since its publication, it continues to attract readers. Many have attempted to account for the novel's continuing appeal, but Paul Doyle, author of the fine Twayne Authors volume on Buck, gets it right, I believe, when he says, "*The Good Earth* stir[s] deep patterns of recognition within the minds and hearts of its readers," giving the "sense," he continues, "of 'being shaped by eternities.'"[1] Thus, despite cultural and chronological distances, each reader feels a personal connection to the struggles and sufferings of the novel's main characters, Wang Lung and O-lan. This essay will begin by identifying some of the more obvious ways in which these connections are established before moving to more extensive explorations of how the author's subtle use of biblical and archetypal imagery and symbolism summons the unconscious mind to draw the reader into the lives and experiences of her characters.

Points of Connection

We can account for the feeling of connectedness in many of the usual ways. First, Buck was an accomplished storyteller. She had developed and enhanced her natural gift by listening to the storytellers on the streets of the Chinese community where she grew up and by her extensive reading of Chinese and English classics. Thus, in her novel she is able to tell a compelling story, one that keeps the plot moving forward in an interesting way and one in which themes, events, and images reflect on each other, producing a pleasing richness, whether one is reading it for the first time or the fifth. For example, the first time the reader comes upon Wang Lung's visit to the House of Hwang to secure his bride, there is curiosity about how their marriage will go. The reader wonders about the prospects of this plain, stolid kitchen slave. The next time, however, the reader is no longer curious. The story and its outcome are well known. So what prompts continued reading? Something else, deeper, beyond the pleasure of the familiar. Later developments in the story—now known—illuminate this moment in a new way for the reader. Things not seen in it before become clear. This plain, stolid slave is transformed in the light of her later accomplishments and sorrows. This moment in the story changes for the reader; in a sense, the book becomes new. Let us reflect on this moment in the novel to see just how this might happen.

In this scene, Wang Lung stands before the dais where the mistress of the House of Hwang is seated. She speaks:

> "Carry her box out to the gate and let them be gone." And then she called Wang Lung and said, "Stand beside her while I speak." And when Wang had come forward she said to him, "This woman came into our house when she was a child of ten and here she has lived until now, when she is twenty years old. I bought her in a year of famine when her parents came south

> because they had nothing to eat. They were from the north in Shantung and there they returned, and I know nothing further of them."[2]

This revelation resonates anew for the reader who knows that O-lan will consider selling her own daughter to get her family back to the farm they have fled because of famine. The mistress's words continue: "You see she has the strong body and the square cheeks of her kind. She will work well for you in the field and drawing water and all else that you wish." This observation is an understatement in the extreme once the reader sees how O-lan's hard work and competence in all matters of farming and domestic living bring prosperity to her household. "She is not beautiful," says the mistress, "but that you do not need. Only men of leisure have the need for beautiful women to divert them."[3] This last remark offers a poignant foreshadowing of Wang Lung's eventual fascination with Lotus. Such richness marks the work of the classic storyteller in which each new reading unearths additional hidden treasures of meaning and emotion.

A second point of connection arises from the author's treatment of fundamental, universal human experiences in moving, unforgettable passages. The novel may be set in the China of prerevolutionary days, but one does not have to be Chinese or know the history of the period to be totally absorbed in the book. All are able to enter easily into the joy and apprehension of Wang Lung on the morning of his wedding day and into the solitary pain and stoic courage of O-lan as she gives birth again and again in situations of escalating tension and deprivation. All readers rejoice at Wang Lung's successes, which enable him to purchase additional farmlands from the Hwang family, and nod their heads in recognition as Wang Lung must find ways to deal with his thieving uncle and restless sons.

Through Buck's considerable powers of description, readers experience the suffering brought on by natural disasters and the heart-rending plight of refugees. They know the despair that might drive a father to sell his child if doing so will get him back to his land, and they relate easily to Wang Lung's desire for Lotus when leisure, prosperity, ennui, and middle age drive him away from his land and toward the temptations of the city. As Doyle writes, "By watching *The Good Earth*'s pageant of living move before us, we come to know not only ourselves more deeply, but life itself more fully and more comprehensively."[4]

A third source of connection between the reader and the text lies in the ability of the author to create believable, three-dimensional characters about whom we care and with whom we can identify ourselves. Buck's highest achievement here is found in Wang Lung and O-lan in whom may be seen the full range of human emotion and experience. Some contemporary readers have described Buck's characters as cold and impenetrable,[5] and one wonders how they have understood O-lan, who vehemently refuses help from anyone at the House of Hwang when she is about to give birth, or the hot tears of Wang Lung when he is about to give up his land to save his family from death by starvation. Hardly cold, hardly impenetrable, both characters are human to the core, enduring and surviving some very hard times. But one is heroic: O-lan. She has come from humblest circumstances, sold as a child, abused as a slave, regarded as nothing.

In the course of the first half of the novel, she shows herself to be extraordinarily competent, clever, practical, and self-sacrificing. Wang Lung's successes are largely her doing. Because of her talents, her thrift, and her good household management, Wang Lung is able to buy land. She makes several critical decisions, keeping a cool head in the most desperate of circumstances. It is she who counsels against selling the land during the famine and handily takes up begging with the children and grandfather when they reach the city. Sensing that revolution and a change in their fortunes are coming, she prevails upon Wang Lung not to sell their daughter into slavery. And it is she who knows where to look for jewels when she enters the abandoned house of the rich family against whose wall she had built a shelter for her family. Yet she is valued, it seems, only when her illness keeps her from tending the house as she used to do. In almost every instance, she proves herself more steadfast than Wang Lung, never changing in response to prosperity, not tempted to take up the ways of the rich. It is she who holds the family together. And it is when Wang Lung abandons her for Lotus that things fall apart.

Archetypal and Biblical Imagery

All of the above are obvious ways in which the novel proves itself to be a classic, continually relevant and alive in each rereading of it. But other, more subtle devices are present as well—devices that stir our unconscious minds as we read, forging connections of which we may be unaware. One such device is the use of biblical and archetypal imagery. The former may be the more familiar, referring as it does to imagery that evokes scenes from sacred Scripture and, doing so, adds nuance and symbolic resonance to a literary passage. The latter, as described by M. H. Abrams in *A Glossary of Literary Terms*, refers to images, patterns, and character types that appear in literature and works of art and reflect a set of very basic and "universal . . . mental forms" that human beings seem to hold in common and which, when encountered in literature, draw forth a deep response.[6]

Interestingly, Buck is not usually credited with using such devices in her works. In fact, Doyle asserts that the critical neglect of her writing after 1939 stems from her lack of "interest in using myth or symbolism or other elements characteristic of the modern novel." This lack of interest, he says, "gives critics relatively little to analyze and explicate. Her novels do not furnish the layers of meaning and the complexity that modern literary criticism demands."[7] Several years later, Peter Conn, author of *Pearl S. Buck: A Cultural Biography*, affirms this assessment, calling *The Good Earth* "groundbreaking in its subject matter but thoroughly conventional in its techniques."[8] And yet, images and symbols that create multiple layers of meaning do seem to be present, and they begin to appear very early in the novel.

The Good Earth opens on a spring day, Wang Lung's wedding day: "A small soft wind blew gently from the east, a wind mild and murmurous and full of rain. It was a good omen. The fields needed rain for fruition. There would be no rain this day, but within a few days, if this wind continued, there would be water. It was good. Yesterday he had said to his father that if this brazen, glittering sunshine continued, the wheat could not fill in the ear. Now it was as if Heaven had chosen this day to wish him well. Earth would bear fruit." Naked to the waist, Wang Lung lavishly pours precious water into the cauldron and lights the stove, determined to bathe his entire body, which no one has looked upon "since he was a child upon his mother's knee."[9] This scene with its emphasis on fertility, rain, nakedness, innocence, bathing, and marriage contains overtones of scenes from Genesis and the garden of Eden. These overtones effectively link Wang Lung and his bride-to-be with every new married couple, all of the new Adams and Eves who will get their chance in the in garden of life. For them, the world is created anew, and their beginning in spring calls up the hope of the first spring and every spring, the spring of youth and of new life.

Biblical images like this one universalize and enhance other experiences described in the novel as well, including the birth scenes and those depicting Wang Lung's prosperity, famine, travel, and temptation, and they help to create the rhythms of the life cycle to which all readers can relate. One such scene offers a compelling and satisfying illustration. Not long after the birth of her first child, O-lan joins her husband in the fields, taking her infant son with her, stopping when necessary to provide for the child's needs. The description that Buck gives is extraordinary in its total believability and in its mythic and sacred overtones. Here are the madonna and child as few have depicted them:

> The woman and the child were as brown as the soil and they sat there like figures of earth. There was the dust of the fields upon the woman's hair and upon the child's soft black head.
>
> But out of the woman's great brown breast the milk gushed forth for the child, milk as white as snow, and when the child suckled at one breast it flowed like a fountain from the other, and she let it flow. There was more than enough for the child, greedy though he was, life enough for many children, and she let it flow out carelessly, conscious of her abundance. There was always more and more. Sometimes she lifted her breast and let it flow out upon the ground to save her clothing, and it sank into the earth and made a soft, dark, rich spot in the field. The child was fat and good-natured and ate of the inexhaustible life his mother gave him.[10]

Through moving, lyrical prose and mythic/biblical overtones, this domestic scene is transformed into a powerful archetype with multiple resonances in which this individual human mother nursing her child becomes one with all mothers of all times and with them becomes a type of Mother Earth herself, rich and abundant, capable of nourishing all of the children who might spring forth from her. It is a wondrously rich and suggestive presentation of human and divine motherhood, one that contrasts sharply with the earthen gods who inhabit Wang Lung's fields, receiving only cursory and haphazard attention, seeming weak and ineffectual in comparison. This is without doubt a central image in the novel, symbolizing among other things the importance and power of the land in the life of Wang Lung and his neighbors. This land is their true god, and they will sacrifice mightily to preserve it and to reap its rewards.

Water is another important biblical and archetypal image that Buck uses well to communicate the universality and sacredness of human experience. It appears at critical junctures along the plot line, helping the author to connect her characters to the broad spectrum of humanity while creating the natural environment of the province in China where *The Good Earth* is set. Wang Lung's farm is located in a region where water tends to be scarce except when the Yangtze overflows and subjects the area to devastating floods. Returning to the opening pages of the novel, we get a good sense of just how scarce and precious water is when we read of Wang Lung's initial hesitance to fill the cauldron for his bath, something he has not indulged in, he says, "since the New Year." His father's reaction to "all this washing" underscores the perceived profligacy of this action: " 'Now there is water enough to bring a crop to fruit,' he said suddenly."[11]

The symbolism of the water at this opening point in the story is both sacred and mythic. Wang Lung, a heroic everyman, engages in a ritual bath as he prepares to undertake one of the great adventures of adulthood—married life and the responsibilities that it brings. The talk of impending rain and its promise of fertile fields and rich harvests symbolically places Wang Lung in the Old Testament garden of Eden where, as a type of Adam—newly cleansed and blessed by the water—he goes in search of his Eve.

Buck continues to use water imagery in this work, exploring the full range of its possibilities and ambiguities. Following his marriage to O-lan, Wang Lung is blessed with abundant rains that ensure rich harvests for several years, and his family prospers. But nature's fickleness eventually leads her to withdraw the rains, and drought produces crop failure and famine. Wang Lung and his family must flee to the city to survive. The saving power of water is revealed as Wang Lung, now a rickshaw driver, escapes conscription into the revolutionary army by taking refuge among the vats in the shop of a hot water seller. Having retained his freedom, Wang Lung is able to return to his land and to prosperity. But as he enters middle age, water, in the form of a symbolic flood, pushes him away from the garden toward the temptations of the city and the charms of Lotus, the sing-song girl. The scene of this temptation is well worth quoting here. It contrasts sharply with the novel's opening emphasis on cleansing baths and fructifying spring rains in its evocation of idleness, indolence, restlessness, and desire.

> But the waters lay placid and unmoved except for the slight summer wind that rose at sunset, and the old man dozed and the two boys trudged to school at dawn and were away until evening and in his house Wang Lung was restless and he avoided the eyes of O-lan who looked at him miserably as he went here and there and flung himself down in a chair and rose from it without drinking the tea she poured and without smoking the pipe he had lit. At the end of one long day, more long than any other, in the seventh month, when the twilight lingered murmurous and sweet with the breath of the lake, he stood at the door of his house, and suddenly without a word he turned abruptly and went into his room and put on his new coat, even the coat of black shining cloth, a shining almost as silk, that O-lan made for feast days, and with no word to anyone he went over the narrow paths along the water's edge and through the fields until he came to the darkness of the city gate and through this he went and through the street until he came to the new tea shop. There every light was lit, bright oil lamps which are to be bought in the foreign cities of the coast, and men sat under the lights drinking and talking, their robes open to the evening coolness, and everywhere fans moved to and fro and good laughter flowed out like music into the street. All the gayety which Wang Lung had never had from his labor on the land was held here in the walls of this house, where men met to play and never to work. Wang Lung hesitated upon the threshold. . . . And he might have stood there and gone away . . . but there came out of the shadows on the edge of the light a woman who had been leaning idly against the doorway.[12]

Symbolic Devices

Water, earth, garden—all are the natural and symbolic elements that make up the setting of Buck's prize-winning novel. They create the natural environment of farm life worldwide and communicate the universality of humankind's relationship with the earth. They are accompanied and enhanced by another rather spectacular set of symbolic devices that appear throughout *The Good Earth*—that of gates, doorways, walls, and windows.

Gates and walls serve as important archetypal symbols in the earliest literature that we have, appearing at critical points in the classical journey of the hero as he undergoes the adventures of separation, initiation, and return described by Joseph Campbell and others.[13] In the Mesopotamian epic of *Gilgamesh*, for example, the hero must pass through a set of gates guarded by lions and the scorpion monsters as he journeys in search of immortality. Upon returning to his home city of Uruk, he constructs a mighty wall on which he records the story of his travels. Allusions to the gates of heaven and the gates of hell are familiar, as are references to the walls of Troy and Jericho.

Chinese mythology includes gods of walls and moats. Named *Chenghuangshen,* these gods, also called City Gods, controlled the ravages of beasts that might destroy the harvest, broke droughts, halted excessive rain, and brought peace and prosperity to the territory over which they presided. Door guardians were even more common. These spirits seized demons that harmed people and handed them over to were-tigers for destruction. Pictures of these guardians were often hung or pasted on either side of doors to invoke protection.[14]

Structures such as gates and walls are ubiquitous in China, as anyone who has been there can testify, so the reader is not surprised to find them as part of the novel's landscape. What does surprise, however, is the way the author uses these structures beyond mere scene setting. First, Buck uses them to create the architecture, the organizational framework, of the action and, second, they provide a mythic underpinning through a set of archetypal images.

Structurally, gates, windows, and walls are used to shape and organize the action of the novel. Each appears at a critical moment in the plot to signal changes in action and development in character. As the novel begins, Wang Lung awakens and tears away the rice paper at his bedroom window, letting in the spring morning and the beginning of his new life as a married man. This gesture initiates the action for Wang Lung and the reader as both look out of the window at the journey into adult life that is about to unfold.

Leaving his father behind, Wang Lung walks to the city alone and enters its gates, realizing that when he comes through them again, he will be changed for, as he notes, "there would be a woman walking behind him."[15] The monumental nature of this change is signaled most dramatically by the next gate through which Wang Lung ventures—the intimidating gate, with its mocking gatekeeper and stone lions, that stands before the House of Hwang. Beyond this gate lie Wang Lung's encounter with his new bride, the beginning of their married life, the birth of their first son, and the prosperity of their first year. Importantly, Wang Lung and his bride leave the House of Hwang, not by the intimidating front gate but by a side gate known to O-lan, saving Wang Lung from the chance of any further embarrassment by the gatekeeper and cleverly foreshadowing the practical gifts that O-lan will bring into his life. Wang Lung's next appearance at the gate of the House of Hwang takes place at the New Year and allows the author to present a touching and triumphant display of the good fortune that has visited Wang Lung and his family and to suggest that the House of Hwang is entering a period of decline.

Through this gateway, Wang Lung and his family move into a prolonged period of prosperity and growth, including the purchase of new lands and the births of several children. This is followed by famine and the move to the south to avoid starvation. As Wang Lung and his family make their desperate journey to the south, they come once again before the gate of the House of Hwang. This time, they do not enter it, for it has been locked fast against the fleeing refugees, but it marks their and the reader's entry into the next major action, their exile in the southern city.

The action in this part of the novel is circumscribed by walls and punctuated by gates that do not open for Wang Lung. Arriving in the city with many other refugees, Wang Lung purchases mats that O-lan turns into a humble dwelling for the family, setting it against a wall that surrounds the land and house of a wealthy city family. Wang Lung takes a job as a rickshaw driver, daily transporting Chinese and foreign men and women to the gates of buildings and houses of pleasure that are closed to him. This section of exile ends when the invasion of a revolutionary army incites the peasants who inhabit the huts along the wall to breach the wall, rush through the gates, and loot the premises. Wang Lung and O-lan are among these looters, and their leap over the wall and through the gates propels them into the next phase of their lives and the reader into the next section of *The Good Earth*. In this next section, Wang Lung and O-lan, aided by the gold and jewels taken from the house in the south, rebuild their lives as farmers, adding many fields. O-lan gives birth again, this time to a set of twins. Their older children must be educated and placed in useful occupations. Marriages must be looked into. Most significantly here, a flood brings on a long period of idleness for Wang Lung. Unable to go to his fields, he grows bored, becomes critical of O-lan's appearance and manners, and eventually strays from the farm to the city, where he begins a relationship with Lotus, an entertainer in a tea house, who will become his concubine. To open this new phase of his life, Wang Lung once more passes through the city gates, this time at night, the time of desire.

Beyond this gate, the reader encounters the family problems that naturally arise with the introduction of a second woman and her servant into a household, including O-lan's displeasure, squabbles over money, "turf wars," and the eldest son's growing interest in his young and pretty stepmother. But all of these become rather insignificant when O-lan falls ill and begins to decline, and this section ends with the longed-for marriage of her eldest son and O-lan's death and funeral.

Two last sets of gates and walls remain. Following the death of O-lan, the Wang family takes up residence within the old House of Hwang, available now because of its owners' need for money to support their severe opium addiction. The gate and walls that once intimidated the young Wang Lung are now his own and mark the final phase of his life—old age. During this phase, he will have to deal with the complexities of the growing families of his sons, daughters-in-law, and grandchildren, and he will develop a late romance with a young serving girl named Pear Blossom. Having put to rest the problem of his thieving uncle by means of opium, he will encounter a new challenge from his nephew, now a soldier with a new revolutionary army that for a time takes up residence in Wang Lung's courts. Eventually, the gates and walls that Wang Lung once coveted begin to oppress him and he flees them, choosing to live instead at the old farm in the company of his mentally handicapped daughter and Pear Blossom, with whom he maintains an affectionate but platonic relationship after their short and passionate interlude. The last set of walls and gates referred to in the novel anticipates Wang Lung's demise. These are the walls of his coffin and the gate of the family cemetery, where he will lie in death, surrounded by the earth that he has loved.

The gates and walls that structure *The Good Earth* serve as interesting entryways into the various courts of the unfolding plot, but they have another important function—that of universalizing the experiences of the characters through archetypal images that evoke common responses from readers.

Gates often signal the heroic rite of passage into a new phase of human experience. Thus, it is not surprising that when Wang Lung goes to pick up his bride, he must first pass through the gate at the House of Hwang: "He stood at the gate for a long time, looking at it.

It was closed fast, two great wooden gates, painted black and bound and studded with iron, closed upon each other. Two lions made of stone stood on guard, one at either side. There was no one else. He turned away. It was impossible."[16]

Seeing the formidable gate, Wang Lung is completely intimidated by it. He feels faint and decides to eat a little before he approaches the gate again. His return to the gate after a meal of noodles and tea is described by Buck in language that is both humorous and mythic:

> This time, since it was after high noon, the gates were ajar and the keeper of the gate idled upon the threshold, picking his teeth with a bamboo sliver after his meal. He was a tall fellow with a large mole upon his left cheek, and from the mole hung three long black hairs which had never been cut. When Wang Lung appeared he shouted roughly, thinking from the basket that he had come to sell something.
>
> "Now then, what?"
>
> With great difficulty Wang Lung replied, "I am Wang Lung, the farmer."
>
> "Well, and Wang Lung, the farmer, what?" retorted the gateman, who was polite to none except the rich. . . .
>
> "I am come—I am come—" faltered Wang Lung.
>
> "That I see," said the gateman with elaborate patience, twisting the long hairs of his mole.
>
> "There is a woman," said Wang Lung, his voice sinking helplessly to a whisper. In the sunshine his face was wet.
>
> The gateman gave a great laugh.
>
> "So, you are he!" he roared. "I was told to expect a bridegroom today." . . .
>
> At last Wang Lung said with anxiety,
>
> "Shall I go alone?"
>
> The gateman affected a start of horror. "The Old Lord would kill you!"

> Then seeing that Wang Lung was too innocent he said, "A little silver is a good key." . . . With his face burning and his head bowed, he walked through court after court, hearing that voice roaring ahead of him. . . . Then suddenly when it seemed to him he had gone through a hundred courts, the gateman fell silent and pushed him into a small waiting room.[17]

One cannot overlook the fairytale, mythic character of the scene. The hero/protagonist, very much in the manner of Campbell's archetypal hero, experiences a life-changing moment, a young man's rite of passage. He has left behind his childhood and prepares to pick up the responsibilities of an adult. Before he can attain his bride and his future, he must get past the gate with its lions and monstrous gatekeeper. He must offer a silver bribe to the guard, a kind of magic key that lets him pass through the one hundred courts before he arrives at the room of his audience with Madame Hwang. There he crosses the threshold into a new realm, the realm of the unfamiliar, as described by Campbell, where he must overcome the power of darkness in the person of Madame Hwang.[18] She sits on a dais smoking opium, Wang Lung's fate in her withered hand. Wang Lung emerges victorious from this adventure, his new bride in tow, having gifted her with several green peaches as a sign of his newly won power.

When Wang Lung visits the House of Hwang for the second time, about a year later, he is accompanied by O-lan and his newborn son:

> Then Wang Lung had his reward at the great gate of the House of Hwang, for when the gateman came to the woman's call he opened his eyes at all he saw and he twirled the three long hairs on his mole and cried out,
>
> "Ah, Wang the farmer, three this time instead of one!" And then seeing the new clothes they all wore and the child who

> was a son, he said further, "One has no need to wish you more fortune this year than you have had in the last." . . .
>
> The gateman was impressed with all he saw and he said to Wang Lung, "Do you sit within my wretched room while I announce your woman and son within."[19]

This time the description of the gate is much less fearsome and mysterious. It is merely a "great" gate, and the gatekeeper is merely a gatekeeper who is clearly impressed with Wang Lung's prosperity and quickly offers him his meager hospitality while O-lan goes to show off her child to those within the great house. No fairytale elements appear. All is within the realm of the real and possible for Wang Lung, whose passage into maturity is marked here.

The third sighting of the Hwang gate appears during Wang Lung's flight from starvation during the famine:

> They were close to the gate of the great house now, but it was locked fast, the iron doors reared full to their height and the stone lions grey and windbitten on either side. Upon the doorsteps lay cowering a few dingy shapes of men and women who gazed, famished, upon the closed and barred gate, and when Wang Lung passed with his miserable little procession one cried out in a cracked voice, "The hearts of these rich are hard like the hearts of the gods. They have still rice to eat and from the rice they do not eat they are still making wine, while we starve.[20]

These gates are a far cry from those that intimidated the young and inexperienced bridegroom. Here there is no gatekeeper who might be bribed to let one enter, no opportunity to cross the threshold into a new realm where opportunity may be won. These are the gates of misery, locked fast against the poor and starving. Wang Lung will get no help here. He must pass by and hope to survive. The gates and walls of the rich are obstacles and challenges to the hero, who is forced to make his way as a refugee in a new city.

When Wang Lung and his family settle in the southern city, they find some degree of security and a subsistence-level existence within the city walls. But other walls, inside the city, effectively symbolize the difficulties endured by the poor as they attempt to achieve dignified, secure lives. Wang Lung and O-lan build a shelter of mats that clings to the walls surrounding the house of a rich family. While O-lan and the children beg on the streets, Wang Lung wears himself out with backbreaking labor as a rickshaw driver. Every day he carries passengers to the gates of rich houses and fancy office buildings but never enters them himself. Instead of scaling these walls and entering the gates, thereby achieving the prize that lies within them, Wang Lung and his family are effectively shut off from economic opportunity. They cling to the walls like "fleas to a dog's back," a symbolic rendering of their slip into subhuman status:

> And at night he knew that he drew men to big tea houses and to places of pleasure, the pleasure that is open and streams out upon the streets in the sound of music and of gaming with pieces of ivory and bamboo upon a wooden table, and the pleasure that is secret and silent and hidden behind the walls. But none of these pleasures did Wang Lung know for himself, since his feet crossed no threshold except that of his own hut, and his road was always ended at a gate. He lived in the rich city as alien as a rat in a rich man's house that is fed on scraps thrown away, and hides here and there and is never a part of the real life of the house.[21]

The walls of the rich are eventually breached when the revolution encourages the refugees from the shacks to enter the courts of the rich house. The bugs that had clung to the walls do their work of erosion and deterioration. Wang Lung ends up with a treasure of gold when he surprises one of the house's last inhabitants as he tries to escape, but it is O-lan who symbolically brings the wall down as she removes a brick from the wall of an inner chamber to disclose a cache of jewels that will set her family on the road to prosperity. This prosperity will lead Wang Lung to acquire the House of Hwang. The very walls that shut him out when he was young and poor and the gate that once intimidated him become his very own.

Near the end of the story, Wang Lung makes a visit to his old farm. Here is the enclosed cemetery where his parents and O-lan lie. Wang Lung reflects on his own coming death and orders his coffin, a final set of walls, to be placed inside the enclosed cemetery, the final gateway of his journey through life.

The archetypal resonance of the images explored above is clear, and in that resonance we connect to the characters of Buck's novel on a deep, subconscious level. Our lives, like that of Wang Lung, may be viewed as a series of gates that open and close, as walls that shut us out or close us in. Buck's use of such images, as much as anything else in the novel, helps make *The Good Earth* a modern classic, likely to endure for many decades to come and worthy of close, continuing, critical scrutiny.

NOTES

1. Paul Doyle, *Pearl S. Buck,* rev. ed. (Boston: Twayne, 1980, 31).
2. Pearl S. Buck, *The Good Earth,* ed. Peter Conn (1931; repr., New York: Washington Square Press, 1994), 17–18.
3. Ibid., 18.
4. Doyle, *Pearl S. Buck,* 38.
5. Ziauddin Sardar and Frances S. Saunders, "China Syndrome," *New Statesman* 22 (May 2000): 46–48.
6. M. H. Abrams, *A Glossary of Literary Terms,* 6th ed. (Forth Worth: Harcourt Brace Jovanovich, 1985), 224.
7. Doyle, *Pearl S. Buck,* 149.
8. Peter Conn, *Pearl S. Buck: A Cultural Biography* (Cambridge: Cambridge University Press, 1996), 124.
9. Buck, *Good Earth,* 1–2.
10. Ibid., 41.
11. Ibid., 5, 4.
12. Ibid., 178–79.
13. Joseph Campbell, *The Hero with a Thousand Faces* (New York: Pantheon Books, 1949), 30.
14. Anthony Christie, *Chinese Mythology* (London: Hamlyn, 1968), 119.
15. Buck, *Good Earth,* 9.

16. Ibid., 11.
17. Ibid., 14–16.
18. Campbell, *Hero,* 30.
19. Buck, *Good Earth,* 49.
20. Ibid., 90.
21. Ibid., 97, 107–8.

CHAPTER 9

"Not Having to Be Alone Is Happiness": The Cal Price Writing Workshops at the Pearl Buck Birthplace as Catalysts for a Glocal Writing Community

Rob Merritt

"Glocal" means something like what transpires in a particular community is both influenced by and an influence on happenings in other communities around the world.[1] That is an inspiring conception to me, and I believe to others who live in West Virginia. As Jim Wayne Miller's "Brier," aware of the dangers of tunnel vision and limited horizons, says, "You don't live the way your foreparents lived. . . . You don't have to think ridge-to-ridge, / the way they did. / You can think ocean to ocean."[2] Pearl Buck's life in China, infused by her love for the plateaus of Pocahontas County, lends a striking energy to her homestead in Hillsboro, West Virginia, a nexus of light that refuses to be extinguished. Since 2012, The Pearl S. Buck Birthplace Foundation has sponsored writing workshops beside the Stulting house where Buck was born in the Sydenstricker cabin (the birthplace of her father, Absalom, moved from Ronceverte, West Virginia) as part of the Calvin W.

Price Appalachian Enrichment Series. I would like to consider how Buck's bond with China creates a snapshot in Hillsboro of how an awareness of Chinese culture leads to a global sense of place, which has been a significant aesthetic influence on a number of contemporary Appalachian writers (including myself). I then want to share what the presenters of the Cal Price workshops since 2012 have had to say about Buck's foundational inspiration for a current generation of West Virginia authors.

I had the opportunity to offer a workshop in 2015. I was first interested in the birthplace because I have been to China, where I taught poetry at the Jiangsu Second Normal University in Nanjing, and saw the house where Buck lived when she taught at Nanjing University from 1920 until 1933. When I read what Buck wrote in 1965 in her book about the place where she was born, *My Mother's House*[3]—"May it live again, my mother's house, and may it prove for others, too, a gateway to new thoughts and dreams and ways of life!"—I knew a component of that gateway to the new had to involve Chinese traditions that could offer ways for residents and writers of Appalachia to see their place anew. The house has hosted visitors from China and is becoming a place for cultural exchange. I took for part of my title a quotation from an eighth-century Chinese poet ("Not having to be alone / is happiness") because sometimes the feeling of isolation in these mountains is overwhelming. Thinking about Buck and the China legacy that she brought to America and especially to West Virginia lessens that isolation. The birthplace has had the same effect on visitors as Buck's mother, Carie, had on her Chinese women friends as recounted in *The Exile*: "they are part of a great and wonderful universe."[4]

Hillsboro is a place we can think of as a sacred China-infused glocal community embodying the essence of poetry as demonstrated by the elements of the Chinese ideogram for poetry (following page):

詩

Here is how to read the characters:

1. the little box on the lower left means “a mouth.”

2. The pictograph above it, four stylized lines, represents indeed spoken lines: so combined, the two pictographs represent a mouth “speaking its lines.” Read together, the “mouth speaking its lines” means “to say.”

3. The ideogram on the upper right—the one that looks like a little cross on a flat base—means “earth.” Originally it was a picture of a flower sprouting from the earth. It transmutes to the word for “place.”

4. In the lower right corner was originally a picture of a hand with a dot measuring how far the pulse is from the wrist. That picture was squared off to mean “measure”—both a measure of distance (1.13 inches, the distance of your pulse point from your wrist) and a measure of justice: “law.”

5. “A place where laws are made,” which—in the culture of the time when the writing system was developed—was a temple.

6. So the character for temple (you read this from right to left) plus the character for “say” means “temple-speaking,” which also means “poetry or “poem.”

This "translation" is by Jerri Bell, who attended a Cal Price Pearl S. Buck Creative Writing Series workshop I offered in 2015 about how we might use techniques of classic Chinese poetry in our work as Appalachian writers. I shared the Chinese word for poetry, but I really hadn't done my homework on the meaning of the components of the ideogram. Jerri sent an email to me and other participants that tells this fascinating story of the character's etymology (which was right before our eyes). This exchange of ideas provides a prime example from my own experience of the community and gateway this writing series has fostered.

Believe it or not, the Chinese poets show up in the work of numerous local mountain writers; for example, from "Portrait of the Artist with Li Po," by a former poet laureate, Charles Wright:

He liked flowers and water most.
Everyone knows the true story of how he would write his
 verses and float them,
paper boats, downstream
 just to watch them drift away,
Death never entered his poems, but rowed, with its hair
 down, far out on the lake,
Laughing and looking up at the sky.

Over a thousand years later, I write out one of his lines in a
 notebook,
The peach blossom follows the moving water,
And watch the October darkness gather against the hills.
All night long the river of heaven will move westward while
 no one notices.
The distance between the dead and the living
 is more than a heartbeat and a breath.[5]

George Scarbrough, born on a farm in eastern Tennessee:

Han-shan was a taker of roads

Speaking doubtless in his unrest
Clever and excellent words,
Pronouncing the Way.

. . .

All men tread the same ground,
Experiencing sunrise and sunset,
The same astonishment of first love,
grievous as the screech of grief.

. . .

I've invested a fabled poet
With an immediate presence,
Furnished a good man a good life.[6]

West Virginia poet Edwina Pendarvis observes, "The mountains here look like the mountains of China."[7] Dan Stryk (Bristol, Virginia) in "Luminous Departure—*After a Poem by Wang Wei*" overtly acknowledges his model:

No longer young, I ask for peace. Abandoning
The sharp gaze of a world that leaps and spins.
I've found no perfect way to live, and brood
About once more losing my heart along
This path I've made my life.
. . .
Despite fatigue, I seek to pierce the gloom to find
My way. To find my way along the water's
Wordless flow. How in life to fail or glow?[8]

Clearly the Chinese poets are in this mountain landscape.

I shared some of these ideas with Chinese scholar Berlin Fang, who worked with Eddie Pendarvis at Marshall University in Huntington, West Virginia, and is now director of instructional design at Abilene Christian University in Texas. This is one of his emails that included me and some of Berlin's Chinese colleagues:

> *Dear Professor Liu,*
>
> *Thanks so much for connecting us to Professors who are so much better at answering questions from Dr. Merritt. It is very interesting to learn the connection between contemporary Appalachian poets and ancient Chinese poets. Professor Zhang and Professor Zhu, Dr. Edwina Pendarvis is a poet herself, and she is also a scholar in Appalachia Studies. It is really worth the effort to explore connections between contemporary Appalachian poets and Tang Dynasty poets. If there are reincarnations in the world, I suspect that Tang Dynasty poets are now living in places like West Virginia and Kentucky :-)*
>
> *Wish you a great Spring Festival!*

Before delving more into how this Chinese presence in Hillsboro, West Virginia, has influenced my work, I would like to share what some facilitators of creative writing workshops at the birthplace have said about their interfaces with Pearl Buck's words and actions. Chia Tao's "Not having to be alone" motif keeps repeating. Writers write alone, ghosts of mentors in the wings.

2012

Poet, nonfiction writer, and novelist Jim Minick, currently living in Georgia, came to the birthplace in 2012. As one of his books is about blueberry farming, Minick was especially drawn to the plant life of the place.

Pearl Buck wrote about faraway places, yet she kept her mountain roots. And those mountain roots taught her both beauty and struggle and how the two are inseparable. The twining grapevines that shaded her grandparents' upstairs porch sheltered her, hid her so she could watch the world while she read Dickens and ate just-plucked grapes. But those vines started as tiny seeds and had to twist and climb over twenty feet to find purchase and sun. Pearl Buck's writing and birthplace show us that we are all those tiny seeds, we are all those twining vines that end in sweet fruit.

2014

Meredith Sue Willis offered a Cal Price workshop in 2014. Born and raised in Harrison County, West Virginia, she is the author of twenty books of fiction and nonfiction and now lives near New York City. She emphasizes that often-neglected aspect of Pearl's biography: her deep concern for human rights.

I grew up in West Virginia and had no idea she was born in the state—they didn't do a very good job in those days of highlighting state history let alone writers of the state. I thought you had to pack up and go to New York City.

My presentation at the Birthplace in 2014 was called, "Pearl Buck as a Social Activist." I gave a slightly longer version that December at the Ethical Culture Society of Essex County, NJ called "Rediscovering Pearl Buck." In both cases I emphasized her deep identification with the oppressed and her work with poor Chinese, and then, when she was back in the States, with disabled children, with mixed race children, with civil rights, and a whole slew of other things. I had first heard of her as a Famous Nice Lady, so I was tickled pink when she turned out to have been a regular firebrand, albeit a generally well-dressed and ladylike one. I have been deeply inspired by

> people—often women, . . . —who appear in history as ladies and turn out to have been change agents. Even PSB's worst potboiler novels had a social conscience, and her best work, especially her memoirs of her mother and father, as well as the currently under-rated *The Good Earth*, are powerful works in structure, impact and language.

2015

In September, Parkersburg, West Virginia, poet Sherrell Wigal conducted a one-day workshop, "The Gateway between Yourself and Your Story."

> I was pleased at the attendance that included local people along with others from Pennsylvania, Ohio, Florida and Virginia. Most of the people who attended were fairly new to the creative writing process and most had never attended a writing workshop or were not part of a regular writing group.
>
> I was quite delighted with the sense of a "safe community" that immediately encompassed the workshop and the participants. I believe the location played a large part in accomplishing that sense of security, friendship and sharing. All attendees all participated in the workshop exercises which I presented and everyone shared touching personal writing. I tried to focus the workshop on the desire of everyone to "tell their story" so that others who might read or hear their story could identify and feel less alone in whatever might be going on in their lives.
>
> What satisfied me the most was that as a result of the workshop many of the participants formed their own e-mail writing group "Pearl Buckboard Writers" (which continues today, almost a year later). The vision of Pearl Buck for her birthplace was that it become "a living gateway to new

thoughts and dreams and ways of life." The fact that a whole new community of writers from different locations emerged from the workshop and created a connection and support group, I believe, directly fulfills the vision Pearl S. Buck had for the Birthplace.

Personally Pearl S. Buck has been an inspirational writer and person for me. She reaches beyond her writing to encompass compassion and activism. Her books and her writing style speak to me on a personal level. She writes from a perspective that is both easily accessible and prompts deep thought.

Sarah Elkins, a poet, writer, and marketer living in White Sulphur Springs, West Virginia, offered a workshop in June, "The Gateway between the Human and Natural Worlds"

My workshop centered on my personal writing practice which very much attempts to reconnect the human experience with the natural world. The Birthplace is the perfect writer's retreat. There is a reverence of place and connection to the land at the Birthplace and in Pocahontas County generally that roots me in the present, which is the only place I can access flow.

The writers who attended my workshop wandered the yards around the houses to find inspiration for their poems. Even the indoor spaces were more closely connected to the outdoors. For the purposes of my workshop it was far superior to be surrounded by rich hardwoods and stone masonry, doors that stood open all day and windows that looked out at the mountains. I think immediately of the difference between the earthiness of the Birthplace and the sterility of a classroom with florescent light, white cinder block walls and air conditioning that is always too cold. The Birthplace is a retreat center. Or, at least, it reminds me of the Quaker and Unitarian retreat centers where I have gone on personal writing retreats in the Northeast. I would like to see the Birthplace used more often by writers and for building a community of writers.

2016

Cat Pleska, a seventh-generation West Virginian, a poet, book reviewer, educator, storyteller, and author of the memoir *Riding on Comets,* has a personal angle.

I taught the Memories to Memoir workshop during that deluge that flooded so many. In fact, I was scheduled to teach the workshop at the Sydenstricker cabin, but there was no power in the whole town, so I gave it at the Marlinton Library.

The workshop went well—I had 12 and would have had more but the flooding prevented some from attending. Pearl had magnificent memories of her long time spent in China and a facility to write fiction and nonfiction with attention to the human heart and mindset, the desires we all experience. In that sense, she is inspiration in her technique, but also her sensibilities for the human condition anywhere. That's one of the observations I try to get my memoir students to think and write about. Mere memories do not make good memoir, says my friend and fellow memoirist Jan Gary. Wise way of looking at it. Merely writing memories down is a good start, but then you must interpret them and make something of them. A good story. Pearl knew a good story and wrote many of them.

As for me personally, I credit Pearl Buck for helping me believe that not only could I be a writer, but that someday I might be an author. I tell this story often because it's truly what happened and truly what inspired me. I was in Marlinton as a young teen during Pioneer Days. I was watching a parade when it began to sprinkle. I was short enough to slip under bleachers lining Main Street to continue watching the parade. Many legs dangled in front of me from the seat above, and one pair of legs had varicose veins, a navy satin skirt and old lady shoes. Then I heard the mayor announce: ladies and gentlemen, please welcome West Virginia's first lady of literature, Pearl Buck. And the varicosed legs uncrossed and Pearl Buck stood up. I had been standing directly under the Pulitzer and Nobel winning author. Although I didn't immediately think that if authors have varicose veins they must be real (I had never seen one, however), that fact did seep into my consciousness. I went home and wrote and wrote, without realizing then the deep impact. No matter, I continued and I have Pearl Buck to thank for that gateway into the greatest passion of my life: writing.

Cheryl Denise is the author of two books of poetry, *What's in the Blood*, and *I Saw God Dancing*. She has a spoken word and music CD called *Leaving Eden*. Cheryl lives in the intentional community of Shepherds Field near Philippi, West Virginia, where she raises a small flock of Jacob sheep.

My workshop was titled "What's in Your Blood." Sometimes our own stories are the hardest to tell. This workshop provided writing exercises that pull from our personal/family history. What is the landscape that shaped you? Using the five senses explore memories that open us up to the past and anchor us in the present. We will stretch memories from a beginning to an ending. I will share examples of poets whose writings reflect their history. We will have time to share our work. We explored the need for structure and creativity. How do you wake a sleeping muse? What writing disciplines and structures help you to keep writing?

The Pearl Buck Birthplace is a beautiful place to hold a workshop—it's a simple log home with such history—and in such a beautiful green expanse of land within the mountains.

> Just the drive there makes one's problems seem so distant and unimportant in the vast scope of the earth. And having the workshop sitting around a wooden table in a circle makes you feel connected to everyone's creativity—including Pearl Buck's. I had a wonderful afternoon there and the participants really did participate with all the exercises and the sharing and I'm a richer person for having been there.

Eric Fritzius of Lewisburg, West Virginia, offered a workshop in September. He is a fiction writer, performer, director, teacher, and audio book narrator. He has taught writing workshops in prison settings and is the author of the short story collection *A Consternation of Monsters.*

> Titled "Mining for Gold," the workshop utilized and expanded upon writing exercises I regularly teach in my creative writing classes at the federal prison in Beckley. It's a workshop about using memory mining techniques to inform your writing, whether it is used for fiction or nonfiction. I dovetailed Pearl S. Buck's use of China as a setting for so much of her work, bringing her experiences there to a broader audience back in the states and beyond, with the ability of writers now to use events and setting from their own lives to better inform their work. Part of my pitch is that we are at all times experts when it comes to our own lives and experiences. We can pull memories and the senses we experienced at the time far more readily than events we might have to research or which fall outside the realm of our own experience. And once we've pulled them, we can alter them as we see fit to create fiction.

2017

Marc Harshman, poet laureate of West Virginia, offered a workshop in April.

I am not sure how this notion got started, but I do think somehow, and for far too long, there has been an idea that Pearl Buck was dated, her writing old-hat, her concerns, although worthy, no longer timely, and . . . quite frankly, that is all rubbish. She is not dated, her prose style remains very fine, and her concerns, if anything, are more timely than ever. Now, yes, mind you, we must read her, as we do any great writer, within the context of her time and place, her era. That done, however, and it becomes quite clear she earned every gram of those twenty-four carats of gold.

Additionally, when you look at the whole of Buck's life, especially her activism on so many fronts, she re-emerges, as she should, a champion of progressive values and concerns. She almost single-handedly transformed Americans' views of the Chinese, was a tireless champion of women's rights, adoption rights, and what we might now call immigration reform. And she never forgot her native West Virginia, despite having spent so little time there. She was, as today's devoted caretakers of the Pearl S. Buck Birthplace home and museum in Hillsboro clearly know, instrumental in preserving this special place.

She is, then, clearly a native daughter about whom every West Virginian should be proud.

Fiction writer and professor in the West Virginia Wesleyan MFA program, Marie Manilla, offered a fiction workshop in conjunction with the Little Levels Heritage Fair and Buck's 125th birthday in June.

When I was a budding writer, I searched for subject matter that mattered to me. I have always loved history and cultural shifts, but I hadn't yet figured out how to layer either into my writing without it feeling heavy-handed. Then I read Pearl Buck's short story "The First Wife." Not only did I mourn for the cast-off, old-world, first wife, but I marveled at the commentary Buck was expertly making about the impact of Westernization on Eastern culture. Here was my exemplar of how to make the personal political. Buck simply showed me the tragedy of one country woman whose well-traveled, well-educated, Westernized husband no longer sees her as a suitable wife and mother. She is old-world China, and she has been discarded. Pearl did nothing less than teach me how to make the local represent the global, and that is no small thing.

In my novel, *The Patron Saint of Ugly*, the main character is a girl born with port-wine birthmarks covering her body. Garnet is shunned by her father who cannot get beyond her stains. One universal truth I was exploring is that, for many women, beauty is a commodity. What if, like Garnet, you don't have that commodity? What if you do, but then your looks fade, as they inevitably will? Additionally, in the novel, those who are beautiful often suffer mightily because of their looks. There is a price to pay for commodifying appearance.

My novel *Shrapnel* chronicles one Texas man's journey to West Virginia. Before Bing Butler arrives, his head is filled with all the Appalachian stereotypes one can imagine. When Bing makes it to West Virginia, everything he thought he knew about us is challenged. Bing represents the attitudes of many people outside of Appalachia. I wanted to put skin on those attitudes, and that's when Bing was born. The challenge was to make him a well-rounded, sympathetic character, and not just another kind of stereotype.

And finally, Kirk Judd, who has been instrumental in seeking to keep the Stulting house and the Sydenstricker cabin open and the Pearl S. Buck Birthplace Foundation flourishing, started coordinating these workshops in 2009 and offered a prototype in the current format in 2011. He conceived of, organized, and secured funding for the creative writing component of the Calvin W. Price Appalachian Enrichment Series.

My experience with Pearl Buck as a champion for justice and an influence on me as a writer goes back to high school. I knew of her status as an internationally known author from earlier WV history studies, and in the 8th grade WV Golden Horseshoe Classes. To me, at that age in the 1960s, there were two world-famous West Virginians—Pearl Buck and Chuck Yeager. I read *The Good Earth* during that time, and counted it as one of my personal favorites. I went on to read more about Pearl and her work for social justice and equality and her influence on the world stage promoting understanding among cultures and compassion for the disadvantaged of the world. Kinda struck a chord with me there in that time in American history. I was proud she was a West Virginian. I started writing poetry at that time, too. Her ideas, if not her style, certainly had an effect on my early output.

In college, I took a creative writing class at Marshall University. Our class time was cut short by riots on campus and the Marshall University plane crash. We had to skip over our section on biography. Our instructor simply pointed us to Pearl's books about her parents, *Fighting Angel* and *The Exile*, and told us if we wanted to know how to write biography to read those books. I did, and started to really appreciate the wonderful craft and depth of her literary talent. I became a fan, and have remained one since.

As a poet in West Virginia, I find her themes of wise compassion, respect of family, reverence for the land and recognition of natural and human connection to be easily transferable from her settings in China to here at home. The acumen of paying attention to where you are in both time and place, understanding the interconnectedness of human existence with the natural world, is more readily recognized and appreciated in an agrarian society such as exists in both rural China and West Virginia. The fact that those truths are universal makes them even more important. The rest of the remote, industrialized, technologically addicted societal world should take heed.

When I became involved in the PSB Birthplace Foundation in the late 2000s, I came to know and respect more about her as a social change agent, working tirelessly throughout her life as a proponent for women's and minorities' rights, disadvantaged children, and cultural justice around the globe. What other job does a writer have than to echo those themes?

Judd invited me to offer a workshop in 2015—"The Gateway between Eastern and Western Creative Forms"—several days before Buck's 123rd birthday. I started in the cabin. We then went outside to write. We looked at some Chinese poems. We looked at some China-influenced Appalachian poems like the ones mentioned earlier. I am still just tapping into Buck's work, but I know there is a special feeling on that green plateau where those Dutch ancestors put down roots and built that big white house with four columns.

Here is eleventh-century advice from Wei T'ei about how to write a poem:

> Poetry presents the thing, in order to convey the feeling. It should be precise about the thing and reticent about the feeling, for as soon as the mind responds and connects with the thing the feeling shows in the words; this is how poetry enters deeply into us. If the poet presents directly the feelings which overwhelm him, and keeps nothing back to linger as an aftertaste, he stirs us superficially; he cannot start the hands and feet involuntarily waving and tapping in time, far less strengthen morality and refine culture, set heaven and earth in motion and call up spirits![9]

I also have found very useful David Hinton's excellent anthology, *Mountain Home*, which emphasizes the global orientation, the contemporary relevance, and the down-to-earth (Appalachian?) rhetoric of the *shan shui* ("rivers and mountains") poets. As the book jacket of that work explains:

> China's tradition of "rivers-and-mountains" poetry stretches across millennia, representing the earliest and most extensive literary engagement with wilderness in human history. It is a plain-spoken poetry of immediate day-to-day experience, and yet seems most akin to China's grand landscape paintings. Although its wisdom is ancient, rooted in Taoist and Ch'an (Zen) thought, this work feels utterly contemporary.
>
> The rivers-and-mountains tradition embraces a remarkable range of topics: comic domestic scenes, social protest, travelogue, and sage recluses shaping mountain landscapes into forms of enlightenment. But throughout that range, these poems articulate the experience of living as an organic part of the natural world. And in an age of global ecological disruption and mass extinction, this tradition grows more urgently and universally important by the day.[10]

This ancient consciousness can be a model for poets now. I have tried to write out of that consciousness:

Book Report

I read *The Exile*,
by Pearl Buck
about her mother, Carie,
about the exile she felt
returning home
to the mountains of Hillsboro, WV
every ten years,

an outsider there,
as in China,
changed by China.

That book, out of print,
I found in the library
at the small Baptist college
where I teach.

Did the Baptist librarians
in the 1940s know that
after following her husband, Absalom,
through fetid ghettos of China
and watching three children
die in her arms,
Carie hated Saint Paul?

One card in the pocket
of a 1936 book,
thick manila pages:
Kay Lawrence, Apr. 1, '74.

The same year that I waited to leave college,
scared of Viet Nam,
venerating Kerouac on my back porch,
a Baptist girl in the Blue Ridge Mountains
touched a woman's bittersweet
novel about faraway
on April Fool's Day.

Only the faintest pencil
underlinings. Kay
knew not to mark library books:
"beauty was a sort
of oxygen that gave her
life energy."

At a college where
men wore flattops in '74,
Kay launched her blossoming.
Carie cultivated her "sensuous nature" singing
in the flourishing gardens she made
upon whatever hard plot she found
at the family's evershifting residencies.
And Kay? She underlined
"music is not technique and
melody, but the
meaning of life itself, infinitely
sorrowful and unbearably beautiful."
Did Kay become a piano teacher,
or a weaver of tapestries,
or the wife of a missionary?
Did she finish the book?
Underlinings stop on p. 67.

Carie went to her heaven,
and her zealous husband to his.

One night in Zhenjiang,
men, angry at foreigners and drought,
came to Carie's house to kill her.
Absalom out, she was ready.
Lights on, doors open,
a party with her children.
She offered tea and
cakes to dark men. She had
faith but also trusted beauty, hospitality,
and the innocence of children.
"Fear is what we must dance with."

The men drank tea,
ate, for they were hungry,

and departed,
axes dragging in the dust.

I open dusty
leaves of a book
to sun after 40 years,
feeling Kay feeling Carie, and Pearl
singing the wisdom of exile—
"Who knows,
God may like
laughter and dancing and beauty"—
in the restorative air
of discrete mountains.

And I also wrote:

Returned from China, I Try to Find the Bar We Frequented

Driving through the neighborhood
where we discovered
camaraderie of shared hope
and Taoist disavowal of war
(though we had not read the *Tao Te Ching*).
I cannot even find the block.
It was a tavern on a green,
wasn't it?

We were halfway to dependency
upon escapism from the era that had broken
the Confucian pact:
"govern by moral force"
(though we had not read *The Analects*).

Voyaging forward
upon the river of time

you laughed in your boat,
flunked out of college,
and did all the paperwork to become
a conscientious objector.
Then, football player,
your knees failed the physical.

Now you have founded a company
that helps young people
recover from dependency
upon escape.

I want to visit you
now that we are old, traveled,
and done with indignation.

Do you still live in a town rejuvenated by artists?
Did you have children?
Do you still talk to mountains?
Do you still offer jovial refreshment to fellow travelers?

I wrote that because so many Chinese poems are about friendship and parting and reuniting, such as this one by Li Bai (701–62):

Parting at a Wine-Shop in Nanjing

A wind, bringing willow-cotton, sweetens the shop,
And a girl from Wu, pouring wine, urges me to share it
With my comrades of the city who are here to see me off;
And as each of them drains his cup, I say to him in parting,
Oh, go and ask this river running to the east
If it can travel farther than a friend's love!![11]

These Cal Price workshops have created a community radiating out from West Virginia. Chinese scholars came to the 2016 Pearl Buck conference in Morgantown. Berlin Fang has said the Chinese poets have been reincarnated in Appalachia. More and more Chinese visitors will come to Hillsboro, West Virginia. A Chinese film crew has recently been to the birthplace. "Place" need not be a region of narrow boundaries. People in Florida can care about mountain-top removal. Many Chinese authors felt, as translator David Hinton says, "the universe is experienced in its fundamental dimensions as home."[12]

Pearl Buck wrote poetry, too. This is from *Words of Love* (1974), from "Alone":

I, in my own grave sleeping
. . .
Yet shall I hear, yet see. In whatever place
While my soul presses on to new and lonely birth,
You I shall hear, shall see, though you
Walk the earth.[13]

She is listening and watching.

NOTES

1. The quotation in the title of this essay is from Chio Tao, "Auspicious Arrival of Yung T'ao," in *The Clouds Should Know Me by Now: Buddhist Poet Monks of China*, ed. Red Pine and Mike O'Connor (Somerville, MA: Wisdom Publications, 1998), 35.
2. Jim Wayne Miller, "Brier Sermon," in *The Brier Poems* (Frankfort, KY: Gnomon Press, 1988), 63.
3. Pearl S. Buck, *My Mother's House* (Richwood, WV: Appalachian Press, 1965).
4. Pearl S. Buck, *The Exile* (New York: P. F. Collier, 1936), 299.
5. Charles Wright, "Portrait of the Artist with Li Po," in *The World of Ten Thousand Things: Poems 1980–1990* (New York: Noonday Press, 1990), 34.
6. George Scarbrough, "The Gift," in *Under the Lemon Tree* (Oak Ridge, TN: Iris Press, 2011), 171–72.
7. Edwina Pendarvis, *Like the Mountains of China* (Ashland, KY: Blair Mountain Press, 2003), 8.
8. Dan Stryck. "Luminous Departure—*After a Poem by Wang Wei*," in *Taping Images to Walls: A Medley of Informal Sonnets* (San Antonio, TX: Pecan Grove Press, 2002), 45.
9. Wei T'ai, *Poems of the Late T'ang*, trans. and ed. A. C. Graham (New York: Penguin, 1977), 7.

10. *Mountain Home: The Wilderness Poetry of Ancient China*, trans. and ed. David Hinton (New York: New Directions, 2005).
11. Li Bai, "Parting at a Wine-Shop in Nanjing," in *The Jade Mountain,* trans. and ed. Witter Bynner (New York: Alfred A. Knopf, 1920), 55.
12. David Hinton, trans. and ed., *Mountain Home: The Wilderness Poetry of Ancient China* (New York: New Directions, 2005), xvi.
13. Pearl S. Buck, "Alone," in *Words of Love* (New York: John Day, 1974), 24.

Contributors

Carol Breslin is professor emerita of English at Gwynedd-Mercy University. She earned her PhD in English from Temple University with a specialty in medieval literature in 1978. Her research interests focus on Chaucer's *Canterbury Tales*, especially those that reflect on issues of justice and law; women in medieval literature; and the life and work of the twentieth-century author and humanitarian Pearl S. Buck. Carol lives with her husband in an old farmhouse in Bucks County that once served as Welcome House, a foster care center established by Pearl S. Buck in 1949 to house and nurture unadoptable, racially mixed children.

Jay Cole serves as senior advisor to the president of West Virginia University. He is also a fellow in WVU's Rockefeller School of Policy and Politics and teaches courses in the WVU Honors College. From 2008 to 2015, he served as chief of staff in the WVU president's office. His awards include a Mirzayan Fellowship at the National Academy of Sciences, selection as a young leader in the European Union Visitors Program, a Foreign Language and Area Studies Fellowship from the US Department of Education, and a Harry S. Truman Scholarship from the Truman Scholarship Foundation. His areas of professional and scholarly interest include higher education governance, Pearl S. Buck, science policy, and Dante's *Divine Comedy*. He earned a PhD from the University of Michigan. He is a member of the Pearl S. Buck Birthplace Foundation board of directors and the Dante Society.

David M. Crowe is a presidential fellow at Chapman University and professor emeritus of history at Elon University. His most recent book is *Stalin's Soviet Justice: "Show" Trials, War Crimes Trials, and Nuremberg*. He is currently writing *Raphael Lemkin: The Life of a Visionary* and working on a biography of Pearl S. Buck.

David B. Gordon holds a PhD in history from the University of Hawai'i at Manoa (1997). His work concentrates on modern East Asian intellectual history. His *Sun Yatsen: Seeking a Newer China* was published in 2009. He is the chair of the history department at Shepherd University in Shepherdstown, West Virginia, and is currently researching Pearl S. Buck's views on Japan.

John R. Haddad holds a PhD in American studies from the University of Texas at Austin. In his research, he studies America's historical relationship with China. He is the author of two books, *The Romance of China: Excursions to China in U.S. Culture, 1776–1876* (Columbia University Press, 2006) and *America's First Adventure in China: Trade, Treaties, Opium, and Salvation* (2013). He currently chairs the American Studies BA, MA, and PhD programs at Penn State Harrisburg.

Charles Kupfer is associate professor of American studies and history at Penn State Harrisburg. He has a PhD in American studies from the University of Texas (1998) and is the author of three books, *We Felt the Flames: Hitler's Blitzkrieg, America's Story* (2004); *Indomitable Will: Turning Defeat into Victory from Pearl Harbor to Midway* (2012); and *Something Magic: The Baltimore Orioles 1979–1983* (2018). His research includes analysis of American journalism and literature pertaining to the early years of the Second World War and the United States' changing world role in the mid-twentieth century.

Kang Liao, PhD, the author of *Pearl S. Buck: A Cultural Bridge across the Pacific* and two books translated from Chinese to English as well as the coauthor of five books translated from English to Chinese, has been teaching Chinese at Defense Language Institute and translation from English to Chinese at Middlebury Institute of International Studies at Monterey since 1999.

Rob Merritt is a professor of English and chair of the department of English at Bluefield College in Virginia. He has published the critical study *Early Music and the Aesthetics of Ezra Pound*; poetry in a number of journals such as *Pine Mountain Sand and Gravel*, *Kestrel*, and the *Asheville Poetry Review*; and anthologies such as *Wild Sweet Notes II: Contemporary West Virginia Writers* and *Coal: An Anthology*. He has published the poetry collections *Landscape Architects* and *The Language of Longing*. He has taught poetry in Nanjing, China, and is a board member of Pearl S. Buck Birthplace Foundation. His research interests include Chinese poetry and Appalachian poetics.

T. J. PARK (Tae Jin Park) is an associate professor of history who teaches world history and specific courses mainly on Asia at West Virginia State University in Institute, West Virginia. A Korean by birth, he studied at the State University of New York at Albany and West Virginia University with a PhD dissertation on US relations with China and Japan in the 1930s and 1940s. His publications include "Guiding Public Opinion on the Far Eastern Crisis, 1931–1941: The American State Department and Propaganda on the Sino-Japanese Conflict" (*Diplomacy & Statecraft*, 2011) and "Is Free Trade a Culture-Bound Ideal?: The Philosophy of Free Trade and Its Applicability in East Asia" (*Encuentros*, 2011).

DONN ROGOSIN has had a multifaceted career as a writer, producer, network executive, and head of an independent production company. His public television work includes the documentaries *East Wind, West Wind: Pearl Buck, The Woman Who Embraced the World* (1992), *There Was Always Sun Shining Someplace* (1982), and *Satchel Paige: Defying Time* (2008). He produced for the PBS system *Fiesta Mexicana* (2007), *How to Learn Any Language* (2008), *Weekend in Havana* (2017), and supervised *The Spirit of Brazil* (2010). As vice president of content development for WLIW/WNET he brought many programs to public television, including *Classic American Cars of Cuba*, *Mariachi Spirit of Mexico* (with Placido Domingo), and *Tango: Spirit of Argentina*. He has also served as the president and general manager of PBS stations WSWP in West Virginia and

WMHT in Albany, New York. His career in the public humanities includes chairman of the New York Humanities Council, and service on the board of the Federation of State Humanities Councils and the Pearl S. Buck Foundation. He is the author of *Invisible Men: Life in Baseball's Negro Leagues*, a former commentator for NPR's *Morning Edition*, a Jefferson Fellow at the East-West Center in Honolulu, Hawaii, and holds a PhD in American civilization from the University of Texas at Austin.

Junwei Yao holds a PhD in studies of English and American literature from Shanghai International Studies University (2000). In his research, he focuses on Pearl S. Buck and Sino-American cultural exchanges. He is the author of two books, *Cultural Relativism: Pearl S. Buck and Her Presentation of Chinese and Western Cultures* (2001) and *Selected Papers of Junwei Yao* (2007). He currently chairs the Research Institute of Foreign Languages and Cultures at Nanjing Normal University, China.

Index

Made in the USA
Las Vegas, NV
10 November 2024

11350671R00115